CLEARED FOR TAKEOFF

SCOTT KAYE

747 CAPTAIN

with Judith Nielsen

DEDICATED TO

My mom, who shaped me into the person I am today.
And also to my children, Kenny and Sabrina, who
inspire and make me proud every day.

Standing inside a 747 engine

TABLE OF CONTENTS

INTRODUCTION

In the United States, there are fewer than three hundred Boeing 747 captains. I am fortunate to have been part of this elite company.

My gaze is fixed at the far end of Runway 28 Right at San Francisco International Airport. My hand is perched atop the four thrust levers that control the 438-ton, fully loaded United Airlines 747. I am sitting nearly six stories above the ground. The two-hundred-foot-wide runway stretches two and a half miles in front of me like an endless stretch of highway. I barely see the departure end. The 213-foot wingspan means that six feet of airplane hang over the grass on each side of the runway. The tower controller keys his microphone. "You are cleared for takeoff on Runway 28 Right," he says definitively. I start my clock and then push all four throttles about four inches forward. Once all the engines begin to stabilize, I hand them over to the autothrottle system. I can hear the thunderous roar of the engines' compressors and turbines spool up. I press the two auto throttle switches and watch the four levers advance on their own to the takeoff position. The airplane begins to vibrate as if it were strapped to the booster rockets of

Runway 28R San Francisco International Airport

United 747 taxiing

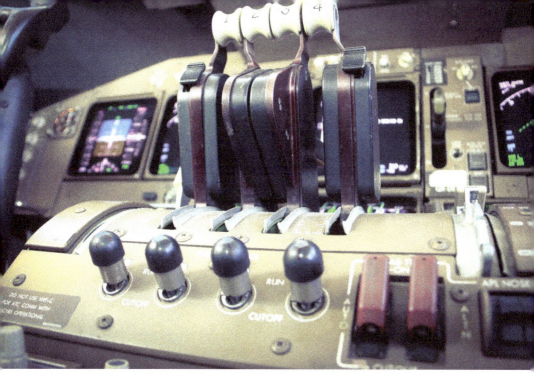

747 thrust levers

the Space Shuttle Endeavor. From the cockpit, I hear the high-pitched whine of the engines, as the 850,000-pound behemoth begins to slowly roll down the runway. Our speed increases more and more until the 231-foot-long aluminum tube strains to part with the ground. With 225,000 pounds of pure jet propulsion pushing us ever faster, my first officer calls, "V1, rotate." My clock shows forty-seven seconds have elapsed since I initiated the takeoff roll. As I gently lift the jet into the air, it displays the grace of a whale leaping out of the ocean, seemingly in slow motion because of its enormity. The two nose wheels leave the runway first. Barely a half a mile later, the remaining sixteen tires leap off the ground in one swift motion. We are airborne.

"Gear up," I command. The gear doors open, the wheels retract into the wells. The gear doors close behind them shielding the belly of the aircraft from the effects of the speed that will follow. In less than a

747 lifting off Runway 28R

United 747 climbing after takeoff

minute, we are over the Pacific Ocean, six miles off the runway. We are on our way to Beijing. As we are climbing out, I silently ask myself, "How did I ever get here?"

Everything I have experienced in my life has led me to write *Cleared for Takeoff* and the other two books in this series, *Trusting Your Autopilot* and *Braving the Elements.* In my story of personal growth through adversity, you will recognize the personal characteristics that will help you scale the hurdles that stand between you and an unimaginable goal. I emerged from a turbulent background and gradually rose to command one of the largest airliners on Earth. If I can make such a leap, so can you. How badly do you want it, and what are you willing to put out to get it? It is not only important that you ultimately achieve the dream, but of equal importance is who you become in the process. I will be transparent so that you can see not only how I did it, but who I became along the way. The traits and characteristics I developed through difficult circumstances allowed me to occupy that seat in the cockpit. At the end of chapters, I suggest you jot down some of the pivotal actions I took to stay on track toward my dream. This list will serve as a template for the journey toward your fondest wish as well. Perhaps my story will help you discover a passion. Human beings need something meaningful in their lives to be excited about every day. The alternative is a banal existence.

Cleared for Takeoff and its companion volumes have been hidden in my mind for decades. Finally, on November 10, 2009, at 4:15 a.m., I got up and started writing. Goals are inextricably linked to adversity. There is no escape from that fact. I challenge you to view adversity as a positive tool. It is the portal through which you may travel, eliminating later regrets for things you did not accomplish. By nature, goals present challenges. I cover many subjects that have touched my life. I will share personal experiences that have caused me to hit uncounted brick walls. At the end of each chapter, I will encapsulate the guidance contained therein. The summaries spell out a roadmap of how to navigate over and around those walls. As you read, put the pieces of the puzzle in place.

We airline pilots have experienced a significant change in both our professional and personal lives, as have many others, as a consequence of September 11, 2001.

I knew Jason Dahl, the captain of the Boeing 757 that crashed into that field near Shanksville, Pennsylvania, on that pivotal day. We were Boeing 737 captains six years earlier. We shared an office at United's Flight Training Center in Denver when our job was to evaluate other captains as well as first officers in the Boeing 737 during their annual simulator training.

I have flown the 757, as well as the 767 that was turned into a missile armed with jet fuel and flown into the South Tower of the World Trade Center.

Conventional wisdom in the psychological community says that real change and growth occur only when a person hits rock bottom. That point differs from person to person. I will share my own rock bottom, and what I learned as a result. I discovered a very real, yet intangible energy that any human being can tap. There is more than enough of this energy to go around the entire planet. This universal energy, if used for selfless reasons, can and will bring anything that you want into your life. You must, however, do the work involved in attracting that energy. Somewhere in that statement is where true happiness lies.

I want to share with you some major events and turning points in my personal journey in the hope that you recognize some of these patterns in your life. I hope this awareness will help you avoid unnecessary personal hell. I sincerely wish to give you tools that were given to me. My intent is that these will lead you in directions and down pathways that will help you answer the questions of life's yet to be uncovered mysteries. This is not a *how to* book, rather, more of an *awakening* book. I have personally found happiness amid chaos. The answers are deceptively simple and obvious, yet concealed. We are not trained to recognize these answers because our parents and teachers do not teach us the manner and form in which they present themselves. Therefore, we must develop that skill set. Getting to my goal was not easy, but then, achievement is never easy for anyone.

I come from a turbulent background with some violence thrown into the mix. Things were ugly in our house. We were living in New Rochelle, New York. My father was a chemical engineer who used to tout his genius quite openly. He worked on the Manhattan Project helping to develop the atomic bomb during World War II. Unfortunately, he grew up in an authoritarian household that made him a very angry person. He disdained women because he thought it unfair that he had to take care of his father who had Parkinson's disease. He so resented it that he eventually found a way to transfer that responsibility to his three older sisters, who in turn developed a deep resentment toward him. My mother also came from a family of four kids and was the youngest. Her family experience was much different. My mother's three brothers, my uncles, were very protective of her. The contrast between my mother's and my father's relationships with their siblings couldn't have been starker.

These myriad differences between my father and mother were a source of constant friction. Whenever my father was challenged or had his buttons pushed, his reaction was property destruction, physical violence on me, or abuse of our pet dog. As a result, I developed an insecurity before I was ten years old. This insecurity fueled my desire to succeed so I could fill that gap. It instilled in me a tenacity that would never allow me to quit once I started toward a goal. Later, very fortunately, that insecurity began to wane as I accomplished more and more. It is fair to say that starting in childhood, I used that negativity as a positive means of shaping my life.

Restraining orders and divorce court battles marked my childhood years. Mom sent my sister, Karen, and me to summer camp in Pennsylvania one summer to remove us from that extreme environment. I said goodbye to Mom and Dad, and off we went. In the middle of the summer, Grandma showed up to take Karen and me out of the camp.

"Where are we going?" I asked Grandma in a puzzled voice.

"We're going to Florida," Grandma responded.

"When are Mom and Dad coming?" I said with concern.

"Mom is going to meet us in Florida," Grandma said.

"What about Dad?" I sounded off in a panicky tone.

"He said he will come when he can," Grandma answered vaguely. I remember thinking, *What the hell is that supposed to mean?*

Later, Mom met us in Florida. Every day I asked her, "When are we going to see Dad?" The answers always seemed ambiguous, as if she was trying to shield us. The real answer: *Never*.

CHAPTER ONE
LIFE IN AN ALUMINUM TUBE

A pilot's job is often far from the exciting work it's made out to be. That reaffirms my favorite expression that people and things are never what they seem. Besides those long stretches of idle time and frequent change of time zones that wreak havoc with one's circadian rhythm, there are conditions in the cockpit that range from uncomfortable to downright miserable.

To handle these routine challenges, I adopted certain perspectives. One was to remind myself how lucky I was to have this job. Not only were the pay and travel benefits great, but the job is relatively prestigious, which is always nice for the ego. I also reminded myself what a phenomenal piece of equipment I was lucky enough to be flying. Still, like passengers, there were times when I wished that phenomenal equipment had just a little more interior space, especially in view of some of the procedural changes that followed 9/11. These changes cause some real Marx Brothers scenarios when the crew is shifting places during the flight.

By approximately thirty minutes after takeoff, the two relief pilots have completed their work and retreat to the bunk room for a rest that may last five to six hours, depending on the total flight time. Before that rest, the relief pilots also usually take a bathroom break. In the meantime, I'm occupying the captain's seat, and the first officer is occupying the right seat.

After 9/11, many safeguards were put into place on airplanes to protect the crew. Among them is the installation of a barrier between the upper-deck passenger cabin and the small space behind the cockpit that houses our bunk room and two lavatories. Before we can leave the cockpit, that barrier has to be locked in place. Additionally, one of those heavy galley serving carts is placed in front of the barrier. During this shift to rest-breaks, all four pilots will be going back and forth between the lavs, cockpit, and bunk room, and it's the flight attendant who opens the cockpit door to let everyone in and out. In addition, the two relief pilots are hanging up their uniform shirts for crew rest in the little closet under which we store our suitcases. These logistics produce a crowded cockpit.

For the flight attendant to open the door to the cockpit, the pilot has to select a code on the wall-mounted keypad outside the cockpit that sounds two piercing alerts. Then the flight attendant inside the cockpit must look through a peephole in the cockpit door to verify that it's one of the pilots entering, and only then can he or she open the door, and never for longer than two seconds. It feels a little bit like being in a kennel. Additionally, there has to be another flight attendant stationed by the barrier to keep passengers outside of the cockpit clear of the area. This whole ordeal in which the crew settles into its positions usually takes ten to fifteen minutes. The process frustrates many flight attendants because it usually interrupts their passenger service. And it doesn't do much for the pilots' moods.

Another minor annoyance for crew, attendants, and passengers is that the inside of an aircraft is generally dry, although the 747 has a humidifier. It uses a massive amount of water, but it works well throughout the entire aircraft, including the cockpit. The humidifier turns itself off two hours before we initiate our descent. As we descend into lower, warmer air, condensation collects above our heads and drips water onto our laps during the approach. Usually, we stuff paper towels in that area to plug the dam. Pilots know to expect this so as a matter of routine, we grab a stack of paper towels from the lav at the beginning of the flight. Of course, that alone can take two minutes, since it feels like the maintenance crews jam those towels into the dispenser with a crowbar.

The artificially controlled moisture levels mean pilots must pay attention to hydration, which is why we're provided with plenty of bottled water. The trick is to manage water intake in such a way as to remain sufficiently hydrated, but not so hydrated that a bunk room break is interrupted by a restroom visit. It's a major ordeal to get out of the bunk, get dressed, call the flight attendants to block the barrier, go to the restroom, come back to the cockpit, go back into the bunk, and try to fall asleep knowing you only have four hours of rest left. The running joke among pilots is that our job is all about "pee management."

A 747 can have as many as eighteen flight attendants on a trip to East Asia, and they too have to rest because of the long flight times. Their rest facility is in the tail of the airplane, at the top of a little staircase where there's a bunk room that holds six beds and two recliner chairs. The attendants take breaks in three shifts of eight attendants at a time. I find it quite amazing that flight attendants can sleep in the tail of the 747 at the lower end of the rudder. Conversely, our bunk room consisted of an upper and lower bunk, with its own door located at the back of the cockpit. When there are four pilots, as there normally are on a long trip, only two pilots are in the bunk room at a time. Generally, I slept in the lower bunk because the bulkhead or wall to the left of our bunk is the fuselage of the airplane and it's more curved in the upper bunk, which therefore feels smaller and more cramped.

Since we were flying at 600 miles per hour, it tended to be very noisy in the bunk, and many guys sleep with earplugs. I didn't because I might miss the wake-up chime from the cockpit, which means one of the pilots will knock on the bunk room door. I hate being awakened that abruptly.

It was especially difficult to sleep in the bunk room when we were experiencing turbulence. I usually instructed the two relief pilots to change altitudes as many times as necessary to avoid such turbulence, but the weather patterns in the Pacific Ocean sometimes make it impossible to find a smooth altitude. If there's anything that will stimulate your bladder, it's lying in a bunk being bounced around like there's a 6.0 earthquake that won't stop. Occasionally, turbulence was so bad that I just gave up trying to sleep, got dressed, went back out to the cockpit, and sat there for the rest of my break.

Sometimes, I found melatonin, a natural substance, to be very helpful with sleeping, but unfortunately it gives me wild dreams. What must be lurking in my head?

To offset some of these annoying aspects of post 9/11 flight, I often reminded myself of what an extraordinary machine I got to fly. I was a 747 captain for the last twelve years of my thirty-one years at United. Of course, I didn't just go aboard a 747 and settle into the left seat. My aviation career stretched for forty years, involved service in 727s, DC-9s, 737s, 757s, and 767s, and included stops at Cort Aviation, Iran Air,

Lloyd Aéreo Boliviano, Emerald Airlines, and People Express.

Well before I retired from United in 2016, I realized what a privilege it was to fly an airplane with the most advanced technology available. Of course, every time United introduces a piece of equipment into the cockpit, pilots have to go to school to learn how to operate that equipment. But training these days is mostly computer-based, and pilots can accomplish it on their own time, using company-issued iPads. This is part of a special program called the United Learning Network, which contains almost anything imaginable to keep us current and to help us review subjects that we feel need "dusting off." It's as vast as a law library, and I have to say, it's pretty good stuff.

The 747 has many features that fascinate me. Among them is a staircase that leads to the upper-deck business-class section, which is just behind the cockpit. This cockpit sits thirty-three feet high when the plane is sitting on the ground, but it's about sixty feet above the ground at touch down onto the runway because of the very nose-high attitude of the airplane upon landing. That increased angle is a result of the flaps at the rear of the wings being lowered to bleed off some speed for landing. Of course, as soon as we lower the nose onto the runway, we're back to sitting at thirty-three feet. I never got over how small people on the ground looked when I'm watching them from the cockpit. At the jet bridge, the cockpit is sitting higher than the airport terminal windows. Because it's easy for passengers to see pilots sitting there doing our cockpit setup, they would often wave at us and sometimes take our picture. Occasionally, I'd even take a picture of them with my cellphone. We smiled at each other, and those holding a baby may wave the baby's hand. It's a lot of fun.

Another fun aspect that helped take my mind off some of these post-9/11 inconveniences were the passengers who are curious about the cockpit and have never seen the inside of one. It was common for them to come up while we were sitting on the ground at the jet bridge, and ask to take a picture. I always invited them in and gave them a cockpit tour, and I even let the kids sit in my seat. I used to also let them wear my captain's hat while mom and dad snapped a picture, but when I stopped bringing a hat, I instead gave them plastic replicas of the metal wings we wear on our uniforms. The kids love to stick those on their shirts. Those wings and my hat must be in hundreds of home snapshots. These are some of the joys of being a pilot that made me grateful when I felt annoyed by inconveniences and stress.

That sense of gratitude carried over to my life away from work. When I found myself getting annoyed off the job, I thought about how many people are walking around out there who have lost their jobs, their homes, and in some cases their fortunes, as a result of the economic crash of 2008. I was very lucky to have kept my losses to a minimum, thanks to the people who manage my retirement plans and, unlike me, really know what they're doing. There's a running joke among pilots that when it comes to investments, we tend to buy high and sell low, however, we make up for it by doing it in volume. Still, I don't think it's any secret that United pilots had their pensions stripped out from under them by a ruthless and greedy executive management. Nonetheless, there will always be those who have it worse, along with those who seemingly have it better. But, do they really? I ask this because things are never really what they seem, are they? The next time you feel a sense of awe watching a pilot striding with confident authority through the airport in his dapper uniform and wings, you might try picturing him with water dripping on his head, being knocked around in a cramped bunk, and trying desperately to hold his bladder.

CHAPTER TWO
A PILOT'S FAVORITE THINGS

All my life, I've loved the feeling of free falling through the air. In junior high school, I was a member of the North Miami Diving Team, which competed with other diving teams in Florida and throughout the nation. I was no good at football or baseball, but I won medals for my diving and learned a great deal about coordination and athleticism in the process. I loved the feeling of dropping through the air off springboards and platforms while performing acrobatic maneuvers on the way down. I've also sky-dived, and I love that as well. On some level, this must be one of the reasons I chose to become a pilot, not for the sensation of going down, of course, but for the sensation of drifting through midair. I love a lot of things about flying too, some that affect me viscerally. One is the view from the jump seat.

When I commuted between San Diego, where I live, and San Francisco, seats often were unavailable on the plane, so I was forced to occupy the cockpit jump seat. Sometimes, I was in an Airbus 320, sometimes a Boeing 737, and sometimes a Boeing 757. The jump seats are vastly different in each of those airplanes. The seat in the 737 has a miserable location between the captain and the copilot, but behind them, and right in front of the cockpit door. In addition to being cramped, the jump seat is hard as a rock. On the other hand, the jump seat in an Airbus 320 is terrific. The Airbus has a bigger cockpit, so there's room to move around when I'm positioning my luggage and getting the seat into position. The seats are also comfortable and well designed. But the best jump seat is in the 757, which is mounted into the rear wall of the cockpit, right behind the captain, and sits even higher than the captain sits. The seat is so high your feet don't touch the cockpit floor, so designers have installed a metal footplate. The windows in the 757 cockpit are large wraparounds that offer an almost unobstructed 180-degree panoramic view. However, the jump seat is so high, I can't see out the two front windows unless I crouch. If I wanted to see during the takeoff roll, I had to look out the side window on the left. Since everything I'm looking at through the side window is much closer to my eyes than if I were looking out the front windows, things seem to move much faster.

It always amazed me how one second we're sitting still on the runway, and then immediately after we're cleared for takeoff we're beginning to roll. I love to watch the side runway lights and the painted lines along the edge of the runway during the takeoff roll. The white lines pass faster and faster until they visually merge into one solid white blur along with the lights that line the runway. It gives me a phenomenal sense of speed. When the pilot rotates, or lifts the airplane off the runway, the solid blur of white lines suddenly becomes terminal buildings, parking lots, and neighborhood houses. I'm still amazed by those ten or fifteen seconds when everything seems to be getting rapidly smaller. Once we reach about one thousand feet, the details fade and a new portrait forms, one that doesn't get smaller quite as rapidly. I love that visual and I'm sure many passengers, even with their more restricted view, love it too.

Another moment I love is sitting on the ground in a plane on an overcast day. I know from my knowledge of weather that overcast conditions occur when cold air is pushing clouds in a downward motion, casting what looks like a sea of white cumulus clouds as far as one can see. It looks almost like a solid white blanket. I know from experience that this layer of clouds lives about one thousand to five thousand feet above the ground and that we'll be breaking through it shortly after takeoff. That's when I can look forward to what I call "skimming." When the plane is actually inside that thick blanket (also known as being "inside the milk bottle"), I can watch as we climb and see the blanket becoming thinner and thinner, the nearer we get to the top. Knowing that, I make plans to level the airplane at the very top of that layer, so that the lower half of the fuselage is in the layer of clouds while the upper half, including the cockpit, is above the layer and we're "skimming" along the cloud blanket like a rock skipping over water. At the same time, we're accelerating rapidly, and the clouds are passing us by faster and faster. It's a phenomenal visual that I have videotaped and pull out now and again in my retirement when I want to enjoy it again. That's not the end of the experience, however, because at some point we have to begin to climb again. By the time we do, the speed of the plane has increased so much that when I pull the nose up to start the climb, the blanket disappears below me at super speed. We suddenly pop out of the top of the cloud layer to a sun that's shining as brilliantly as ever, even though we couldn't see it from the overcast ground below. Knowing that, we always put our sunglasses on ahead of time, even while still in the clouds.

Another stunning visual occurs when a thunderstorm of towering cumulus clouds is building somewhere in the distance, either to our left or right. These cumulus clouds can build very fast, and you can see the column of warm moist air that's rising very rapidly. At United, we were not allowed to fly within twenty nautical miles of a cumulus thunderstorm cloud if we're on the downwind side and not within ten nautical miles if we're on the upwind side. To fly over one, we had to clear it by at least five thousand feet. Advanced radar onboard not only detects an area of turbulence but indicates how severe it is. Light areas show up as green, moderate as yellow, and hot as red. It's very visual and easy to interpret quickly. We can also determine the thickness of a cloud structure by using the tilt function of our radar dish, which sends out microwave energy to pick up the reflectivity of clouds.

Perhaps the most spectacular view from a cockpit, and especially at night, is the northern lights. The shimmering aurora is created when electrically charged particles from the sun enter the Earth's atmosphere and collide. The lights are seen above the magnetic poles of the northern and southern hemispheres and are known as Aurora Borealis in the north and Aurora Australis in the south. Mostly they appear in pale green and pink colors, although shades of red, yellow, green, blue, and violet have been reported. The lights appear as scattered clouds of streamers, arcs, or rippling, shooting rays that light up the sky with an eerie glow.

Another phenomenon of light that I love is known as the "green flash," which occurs at sunrise and sunset when some part of the sun suddenly changes color. At sunset, this change is from red to orange, green, or blue. It's called the green flash because it appears as green for only a very brief moment. The green flash can be observed from any altitude where the horizon is unobstructed, such as over the ocean, but it's also possible to see it over cloud tops and mountaintops. At the equator, the flash rarely lasts longer than a second. I've mostly witnessed it over the ocean where my view of the horizon is at its clearest. I've made many attempts to capture the green flash with a camera but it comes and goes so quickly, it's practically impossible, so I switched to video. Although it's very elusive, there's a way to catch the flash at sunset. Since it's always dangerous to look directly at the sun, you avert your eyes until only the very top of the sun's disk is about to disappear below the horizon, then you quickly glance in its direction.

The green flash

Stunning visuals that aren't made by nature but by man, or something approximating man, also exist. I haven't seen them, but a lot of airline personnel have, including a group at Chicago O'Hare International

Airport back in 2006. On Tuesday, November 7, of that year, federal authorities at O'Hare received a report that airport staff was witnessing a metallic, saucer-shaped craft hovering over Gate C-17. It was first spotted by a ramp employee who was pushing back United Flight 446, which was departing Chicago for Charlotte, North Carolina. The employee apprised the crew of Flight 446 that there was a strange object above their aircraft and there's evidence the pilot and copilot also saw the object. It's unclear whether they "officially" commented on it, and if not, I suspect a reason might be that they were worried about their credibility.

Several independent witnesses outside the airport also saw the "flying saucer," which one described as a "blatant" disc-shaped craft hovering over the airport that was "obviously not clouds." According to this witness, nearby observers gasped as the object shot through the clouds at high velocity, leaving a clear blue hole in the cloud layer, a hole that seemed to close itself shortly afterward.

The *Chicago Tribune* reported that witnesses said the disc was visible for approximately two minutes and was seen by close to a dozen United Airlines employees, ranging from pilots to supervisors, who heard chatter on the radio and raced out to see what was happening. So far, no conclusive photographic evidence of a UFO has surfaced, although reportedly one United pilot had a digital camera with him and may have photographed the event. Where those photos may be is anyone's guess. The conventional wisdom among airline pilots is that if you submit either a verbal or written report about a UFO sighting, you have an excellent chance of kissing your job goodbye and establishing a screwball reputation that will follow you to your grave. Furthermore, no one wants to get embroiled in a battle with a government that has clearly adopted a "denial at all costs" policy regarding UFOs. That's what happened with the O'Hare incident. Both United and the Federal Aviation Administration first denied that they had any information at all on a UFO sighting until the *Tribune* filed a Freedom of Information Act request that uncovered a call by a United supervisor to an FAA manager about the sighting.

The FAA's official position was and is that the sighting was caused by a weather phenomenon, and that it wouldn't be investigating the incident. But UFO investigators who work for The Mutual UFO Network (MUFON), a nonprofit organization established in 1969 to investigate claims of UFO sightings, have pointed out that this decision contradicts the FAA's mandate to investigate possible security breaches at American airports. In this case, that possible breach amounts to an object witnessed by numerous airport employees and officially reported by at least one of them, hovering in plain sight over one of the busiest airports in the world. Many witnesses interviewed by the *Tribune* were apparently "upset" that federal officials declined to investigate it further.

I don't generally subscribe to conspiracy theories, but there are two I can't refute because of the preponderance of empirical and anecdotal evidence. The first is that the shot that killed President Kennedy in Dallas came from behind the picket fence on the grassy knoll, and not the Texas School Book Depository. The second is that the government is aware of the presence of intelligently controlled UFOs, is denying it, and is offering bogus explanations that they're weather balloons or meteorological phenomena. Spare me!

Although I've never seen a UFO, I wish I could say I have. Such a sighting would rank among my favorite "visual experiences" as a pilot, especially since I believe there are many forms of intelligent life out there, and some of them have been here. I can't prove it, but neither can I refute it. I can say, however, that many pilots throughout the aviation world report that they have seen UFOs and I consider them credible witnesses; pilots know the difference between airplanes, weather anomalies, and weather balloons. I remember one flight when a conversation about UFOs popped up in the cockpit, and we talked about how far ahead of us these ETs must be if they're capable of interstellar travel. That naturally progressed to their possible spiritual advancement, which we equated with a species able to survive long enough to attain this level of technology. Then we discussed the fact that in the world of cosmology there is the belief that 225 billion galaxies exist in the observable universe, as indicated by the Hubble telescope. What are the odds of intelligent life not existing on at least one planet, in at least one of those solar systems in one of those 225 billion galaxies?

What extraterrestrials would have been doing at O'Hare is another mystery—were they checking out our latest flight technology? Thinking of making radio contact? Or just enjoying the visuals, as we pilots do? If so, it's something we have in common. Flying into O'Hare or any other airport is another of my favorite visual joys.

The approach to an airport can be easy or hard, but it's always interesting. Some airports such as O'Hare or Los Angeles International are fairly easy because they're near large visual landmarks, such as Lake Michigan or the Pacific coastline, respectively. Other airports are in the middle of large sections of highly constructed and populated areas, and at twenty-five or thirty miles away they tend to blend into the landscape. Even at night, it's difficult because an airport is just another conglomerate of lights merging with the city lights. After dark, pilots have to look for a specialized rotating beacon at the airport that alternates flashes of green and red. Navigation equipment also indicates where the airport should be. Nevertheless, when you hear about a pilot landing at the wrong airport and wonder how that can possibly happen, I guarantee you it's not as improbable as you might think. Sometimes there are two, three, or even four airports within a ten-mile radius and selecting one visually can be a challenge. Crews avoid this by verifying the selected airport with a high level of specificity. Pilots have airport diagrams on approach charts that give each airport's runway configuration, runway lengths, and type of lighting. Pilots confirm that the chosen airport matches the description that's on the airport diagram, then relax and enjoy the view.

One of the bonuses of flying into San Francisco International is that it's right on the breathtaking San Francisco Bay. It's easy to find and is surrounded by gorgeous mountains, water, and green, wooded landscapes. Normally when planes approach SFO from over the Pacific, they're flying along the south side of the airport and the controllers will take them anywhere from five to ten miles past the airport before they turn them back for a visual approach. That puts the plane over San Francisco Bay heading toward the San Mateo Bridge. Pilots know that they should be at nineteen hundred feet by the time they reach the San Mateo Bridge if the descent profile is correct. If there's a fair amount of other air traffic in the area, controllers will keep planes a little higher for traffic separation purposes. That's a challenge—pilots have to get the plane down from a high altitude rather quickly without a large increase in airspeed, which is known as a "slam/dunk" in aviation speak. The part I love is when we start to get within one mile or so of the airport at about five hundred feet, and things begin to move underneath the airplane faster and faster. When that happens, there's a natural tendency for inexperienced pilots to begin to overcorrect the airplane while making minor heading and airspeed changes that may be required. Many pilots with low flight time tend to fall victim to what we call "PIO" (pilot induced oscillation). But when you do these flights routinely, you're so used to the visual reference of increasing speed as you near the concrete, that you know not to do a PIO.

At the final moment, when the aircraft is over the runway itself, the only thing pilots should focus on is the third of the runway farthest away, otherwise depth perception can go a little awry. That's when pilots need to "flare" the plane to cushion the actual touch down before allowing the nose wheel to fly itself down to the concrete (only the main wheels touch the concrete initially, and then the nose wheel lowers itself). To prevent the nose wheel from slamming down too hard, pilots continue to fly it a little bit until it can ease itself down as gently as possible. That whole bit between one mile out and touch down is one of my favorite parts of flying, and it never gets old. I love the feeling of increasing speed with decreasing distance. Every landing is different, and every landing is a challenge, but I could tell by one hundred feet above the ground whether it was going to be soft and awesome (what's called a "squeaker") or not that awesome (known as an "arrival").

There are times when a "squeaker" or soft landing is implausible—such as during a strong crosswind or on a runway that's slippery from rain or snow. Those require different landing techniques in which "holding the airplane off" for a soft landing can create problems, such as hydroplaning or skidding.

Not all the visual thrills of flying are from the air; many are also on the ground. One of my favorites at SFO is when I ferried an empty airplane to the maintenance hangar, known as "The Super Bay," on the other side of the airport. There's nothing like taxiing a 747 up to a gigantic hangar door, much as you would drive your car up to your garage door at home.

Other visuals I don't love at all, but I have to admit they are interesting.

One of those is taxiing the airplane in the immediate area of terminal buildings, where many airplanes sit at gates with their tails and wings jutting out into the tarmac where I'm taxiing, posing the risk of a collision. To prevent that, there's always a double solid yellow line that the sitting plane can't extend beyond, but it's difficult from a distance to tell whether the protruding tail or wing is inside or outside those lines. I depended on my first officers to use great vigilance to help judge that distance.

I've sat in an airplane as a copilot and watched while the captain taxied the left wing right through the side of a catering truck that was outside of the yellow lines. Since it was on his side of the airplane, I had absolutely zero visibility, so the crash was quite a shock to me. Fortunately, no one was hurt, but that captain had a lot of explaining to do, particularly since it was the second time he'd done something like that. I'd be lying if I said it couldn't have happened to a better guy—he was one of those who flew during the pilot's strike at United in 1985 when so many pilots lost so much. I have a hard time forgetting that kind of self-interest.

Another target-rich environment for lively visuals is Narita airport in Tokyo, which has been known to have more Boeing 747s on the ground at any one time than any airport in the world. When we were holding short of the runway for takeoff, it was not uncommon for us to have to wait for two or three 747s or 777s to land before we got takeoff clearance. It's dazzling to see a 747 coming over the threshold of the runway right in front of you, maybe forty feet away. It's impressive, eye watering, and a little scary, but the perspective is unforgettable.

Sometimes after I landed at Narita, cleared the runway, and made my turn-off on to the taxiway, there would be another 747 on the same taxiway going the opposite direction toward the nose of my airplane.

Of course, he's going to turn onto a parallel taxiway before we meet, and ground control has directed him to hold short while we approach the turn for our gate. But that sometimes put us dead center, nose to nose. There's nothing like the sight of another 747 sitting right in front of your face, sometimes so close the two pilots can see each other smiling. Many times it was another United plane, and we waved to each other. Sometimes it was another airline, and when we met, it felt like two competitors facing off at the beginning of a boxing match. We still smiled. I always felt a connection with the guys in the opposing cockpit no matter what name is painted on the side of their airplane. I suspect I'd even feel a similar connection if I found myself face to face with an ET over O'Hare.

CHAPTER THREE
HO HUM MOMENTS

I'm not a person who particularly enjoys wasting time, and I particularly don't like being bored. Whenever I'm idle, and my mind isn't engaged, I have a tendency to get fatigued and to shut down, which often means I fall asleep. I used to do this on the couch watching TV. I would be watching the Kardashians, or something else not the least engaging, but which I watched in the name of being a family man and joining with others around me who liked it. Then suddenly I'd drop into sleep from sheer ennui. People have even commented on how they envy my ability to sleep anywhere, anytime. But this trait isn't a blessing; it's a symptom of boredom. I've never been diagnosed with ADD, but I would bet good money that I have it. I could even get fatigued in the airplane when there are periods of inactivity, although that seldom happened because we were normally kept busy with just our routine.

One thing that did fatigue me was an air traffic control delay. Generally, we got these either at the jet bridge before pushback or in line on the taxiway waiting for takeoff. These delays are mentally trying for me because, like the passengers, I have nowhere to escape the tedium of sitting and waiting. All of us are prisoners in the aluminum tube.

One predictable period of inactivity occurred when we arrived at the plane after doing our flight planning downstairs in the flight operations area. We generally completed the entire cockpit setup in forty-five minutes to an hour, and then sat there for forty-five minutes with nothing to do before we pushed back. Usually, that was a good time to get something to eat in the airport, instead of wolfing it down in the cockpit from lap trays. It was also a good time to check emails and make phone calls before leaving the United States for four days. That also helped me get into a relaxed state so that when I did arrive at the airplane, I was more prepared to deal with any stressors that arose unexpectedly, and believe me, they do in this business.

Still, I would love to have had a dollar for every time I sat in the cockpit as a first officer and heard the captain say, "Well, we peaked early once again," meaning we'd arrived so far ahead of departure that we'd completed the cockpit setup and were now idle. Pilots don't like to be idle; we like to keep things moving forward, and we all know that about each other. The understanding behind the statement "we peaked early again" is that we were in for a period of mutually abhorred boredom.

Roughly thirty minutes after takeoff, the two relief pilots go to the bunk room to rest for about five and a half hours on a twelve-hour trip. The relief pilots, called "bunkies," always go first because if the captain and first officer rest last, they're sharper for the approach and landing. During those first thirty minutes after takeoff, the bunkies are doing administrative work, including planning out the rest periods and making required radio calls. Once they retreat into the bunk room, the dynamics in the cockpit change completely. My first officer and I would find ourselves alone, and it suddenly seemed strangely silent after the chaotic ten or fifteen minutes of bathroom breaks, setting up barriers, and the entrances and exits of flight attendants. Once silence begins, there is not that much to do for a while—boredom can descend rapidly.

Located between the first officer and captain on the center console, or pedestal as it is known, is our ACARS, the Aircraft Communications Addressing and Reporting System. A "time remaining" readout on the ACARS counts down the remaining flight time in one-minute increments. At that point, when everything has become quiet, it wasn't uncommon for one of us to look at the ACARS and jokingly ask, "Are we there yet?" I've been known to turn to my first officer and say, "Well, only twelve hours and five minutes to go." This state of boredom is so pervasive in the airline industry that it's inspired many a joke.

This aversion to wasting time or being idle translates into my everyday life, especially in the way I run errands. I tend to compress them into one part of the day, starting from the farthest point from home and working my way back. Sometimes, I create a memo on my phone to jot down reminders, shopping lists, or anything else. That way I don't waste time the next day doing what I forgot to do the day before. I think most people do this sort of thing, but my own love of efficiency happens to be a result of life in a cockpit—too many chaotic hours followed by too many idle hours.

CHAPTER FOUR
ARE WE THERE YET?

Everything in life seems to be a trade-off, in which we exchange one advantage for another and weigh gains against losses. This is especially true in the professions we choose, none of which are perfect. For pilots, one of the largest sacrifices, and at the same time one of the benefits, is the lack of routine.

In the United States, we generally think of a workweek as Monday to Friday, 9:00 a.m. to 5:00 p.m., but this is a myth in many professions. When I owned a designer furniture business, a step I took as a hedge against unpredictable trends in the airline industry, I quickly learned that there needed to be twenty-five hours in a day. It seems that the more status a profession has, the more demanding it is. In medicine, specifically surgery, your hours can be chaotic simply because you can't predict an emergency. Law isn't much different. I know attorneys who bring briefs home when preparing for a case, doubling their work day. Their profession is their life and in many cases their identity. Businessmen and women can have a real "road warrior" life if their work requires a lot of traveling, although much of that travel has been replaced with video conferencing. Yet few professions are farther from the nine-to-five workweek than commercial aviation.

To airline crews, there's no such thing as a "weekend." A typical trip can take them out of town anywhere from one to nine days, depending on whether they're flying domestically or internationally. And those are days with long hours. A trip to Shanghai from the West Coast, for example, is twelve hours and thirty minutes. For me, living near San Diego, the entire timeline would look something like this:

4:00 a.m.: Get up.

5:00 a.m.: Drive to airport for flight from San Diego to San Francisco, where the Shanghai flight originates. Arrive early in case the first flight is full, and someone senior to me bumps me from the cockpit jump.

7:00–8:30 a.m.: Fly from San Diego to San Francisco.

8:30–11:25 a.m.: Update my company iPad, watch airplane systems videos in the learning library, and talk to other pilots.

11:25 a.m.–12:55 p.m.: Report at 11:25, prepare for Shanghai flight at operations center (complete paperwork, review eight- or nine-page flight plan, current maintenance items, weather package, and special notices).

12:55–1:55 p.m.: Perform a lengthy cockpit setup.

1:55 p.m.: Push back from the jet bridge, start engines, taxi to runway for takeoff.

By the time I've arrived at my base of San Francisco, where the trip originates, I've already been up for several hours, and so have the other three pilots with whom I'm flying. When we "finally" take off, even if no interim problems arise, we're already feeling the first signs of fatigue, given the amount of flight preparation we've completed.

Flight: Twelve hours, thirty minutes.

Arrival: Take hourlong bus ride to hotel in downtown Shanghai.

For a pilot, the hotel experience begins at the gate upon arrival. We gather our luggage, deplane, and walk toward customs. After we clear customs, we go to the front of the airport where there's usually a crew bus or a contracted limo to drive us to the hotel. In Asia, airports are often far from the downtown areas where our hotels are.

At the hotel, we go to a check-in area that serves crew members only. It's not uncommon to run into the outgoing crew as we come into the lobby. This is a good opportunity for a little camaraderie, as well as to brief them on the status of the aircraft they're about to fly. Normally, those arriving agree to meet in the lobby at 5:00 p.m. to go to dinner and have a beer. We all know our favorite restaurants in each city, so we take a democratic vote on where we'll eat and then head for our rooms.

By the time I walk into my Shanghai hotel room, it's been twenty-three hours and thirty minutes since I awakened in San Diego. One of the challenges on a layover is trying not to succumb to sleep as soon as I enter the room and see the bed. If I sleep at that point, I may not wake up in time for dinner. It also means I won't be able to sleep later when I'm on my normal home time circadian rhythm.

Shanghai is fifteen hours ahead of San Diego, so I often lost track of what day it was. That fifteen-hour time disparity means it's a different day in Shanghai than at home. If we took off at 10:00 a.m. on Monday in San Diego, it was 1:00 a.m. on Tuesday in Beijing. When we land, it was 4:00 p.m. on Tuesday in Beijing, but my body thought it was 1:00 a.m. on Tuesday in San Diego. Of course, a similar problem occurred on the return. All international travelers have experienced this sort of time warp—but for pilots, it's a way of life.

We managed the time warp in different ways. Some tried to adjust to Shanghai time, which meant they were sleeping at hours that were a struggle for their bodies. Since we stayed at Hyatt Regency, Intercontinental, and Hilton Hotels, where fitness centers are usually open twenty-four hours a day, it wasn't uncommon to find pilots from various airlines working out at 3 o'clock in the morning. Others, and I'm one of them, would deliberately try to stay acclimated to their home time. To do that, I had San Diego and Shanghai times on my phone to avoid the mental gymnastics of switching back and forth between time zones. But even apps have a hard time adjusting to time differences. In fact, they don't adjust. MyFitnessPal, a nutritional app that helped me log my intake of food so I could maintain my weight, runs on Pacific Standard Time. Consequently, I was never sure whether to log lunch on home time or Shanghai time, or even for what day.

Generally, I set the second time zone on my watch before takeoff from San Francisco. The analog hands stayed on San Diego time, and the digital window was set to Shanghai. The problem was that if I looked at my watch and saw the analog hands at 10:00, I asked myself, is it morning or night? After a couple of days on the road, I would become disoriented.

Setting alarms for wake-up was also a problem. I never trusted hotels for my wake-up call; too often they missed the call completely. If a crew of more than twenty-one people was waiting for me in the lobby for the return to the airport, a missed wake-up call wasn't a luxury I could afford. Thus, I turned to my phone as a backup. I was never sure whether the alarm was set to home time or my current geographic location, and I was always relieved when it went off when it should.

By the end of a three-day trip, I was completely drained, and it didn't seem to matter how much sleep I had during a layover. It was never enough. I preferred layovers of less than thirty hours, not only because they were less disruptive to the circadian rhythm, but because long layovers got boring. I would always rather be home . . . especially after thirty years of layovers.

There were benefits to this time-jumbled lifestyle. Often, I was home during the week and could run errands when there were no crowds or traffic. Sometimes I forgot what a luxury that was until I found myself trying to get to the mall in Saturday bumper-to-bumper traffic. The downside was leaving my home on a Saturday, all dressed up in my uniform and preparing for a commute to San Francisco and a three-day flying trip, while my friends were organizing a barbecue, party, happy hour, or maybe a bike ride. In the end, I liked my unconventional schedule, or I wouldn't have chosen this profession. Furthermore, it provoked some deep thinking about time itself, what it is, and how we perceive it.

I tend to think of time in terms of physics, and that our view of past and future is limited by our five senses. To me, time is illusory, an impression that is especially strong when I'm crossing multiple time zones, and hours and days seem to run together into one simultaneous moment.

Behind every worker is a philosopher of some kind, and pilots are no exception.

CHAPTER FIVE
ACT AND YE SHALL RECEIVE

I believe that abundance, not scarcity, is the law of the universe and that abundance gravitates to those who *take action*. This has been proved to me over and over again in my career, starting way back when I was first dreaming of becoming a pilot and especially when I started looking for very competitive positions within the airline industry.

When I was first applying to the major airlines, in 1975, there were maybe fifty thousand applicants for just a few pilot positions. It was a frustrating and impersonal world where your fate lay in the hands of indifferent workers in the almost mythical HR department. That's when I decided to create my own fate.

Conventional wisdom at the time was that if you bombarded the employment office with resumes and application updates, it would only annoy them and they'd shove your application into the inactive file. The trick was to get an interview without provoking them and hope your application somehow landed in the "to be considered" file instead of the "never in a million years" file.

After years of application updates with no interviews, I did a crazy thing. I put on a suit, flew to Atlanta where Delta's employment office is located, walked in unannounced, and asked if they could tell me what the status of my application was. I knew it was presumptuous, and that I could have jeopardized any possibility of an interview, but I figured, "What do I have to lose? I'm not getting any interviews anyway." So instead of passively waiting, I decided to act.

Several months later, Delta called me for an interview. I don't know if it was coincidence, but I choose to believe that the woman I confronted that day in the employment office silently respected my initiative. I think she placed my application in a special file that later led to an interview. Had I followed the "conventional wisdom" and not asserted myself, I would never have made that trip to Atlanta and might still be waiting for a phone call.

Action can take many forms, and it can often be internal as well as external. Take visualization, for example. I've found visualization to be a powerful mechanism for keeping me engaged and getting results. In those years while I worked toward becoming a pilot, I would visualize myself wearing the uniform, flying the plane, and living the lifestyle of a pilot. Many times, feeling dejected and tempted to quit, those images were the only thing that propelled me. Quitting, after all, guarantees failure, so whatever tool can keep us motivated is invaluable. Visualization can't replace effort, but together they make a dynamic duo that almost guarantees success. I began visualizing in the earlier stages of my career, even when I was still a flight instructor, but I never let up on external action, some of which could even have been described as audacious. This was especially true of the time I decided I wanted to fly a Learjet.

In the world of corporate jets, the Learjet reigns supreme, a plane that is the epitome of speed and power. The Learjet was distinctive from its start. Bill Lear modeled the plane after a Swiss fighter jet and the engines on the older Learjet 25 series are the same ones that were used on the U.S. Air Force fighter jet trainer, the T-38. The Lear can climb initially at more than seven thousand feet a minute, just like a shuttle launch out of Cape Canaveral. It can reach an altitude of 51,000 feet, higher than most airliners can go, and it has a top cruising speed of over 500 mph or Mach .82, which is getting close to supersonic. Simply put, the Learjet can get you there faster. You can also bring along about eight friends.

Learjet climbing

It's no wonder that flying a Learjet is the fantasy of many a would-be pilot, and I was no exception. But unlike most, I had the chance to do it.

While I was working as a flight instructor in Cessna planes, the first stop in my aviation career, one of my best friends was lucky enough to get a job as a copilot at a Lear charter company out of Fort Lauderdale International Airport. (Later, he was the copilot on the flight on which Howard Hughes died, but that's another story.) Piloting a Learjet was a highly coveted job that usually went to friends and relatives of the owners of the company. I was neither, and it drove me crazy. I hung around, trying to get to know people and become one of those lucky "friends," so that when there was an opening, people would remember me. I even took a job there in 1975 as a fueler and airplane washer in hopes of backseating my way into a copilot job. For six months I drove myself nuts watching all these guys pull onto the ramp in these gorgeous "biz jets," then emerge in natty business suits, while I was covered in fuel and grease from head to toe.

The whole situation was made worse by the fact that my boss, George, knew what I was trying to do and hated me for it. I viewed myself as a pilot masquerading as a ramp guy, and it showed. George, in excellent crab-basket fashion, used to scrutinize me from across the hangar, just waiting for me to screw up so he could validate his antipathy toward me. I played right into his hands.

One day, I was towing a million-dollar Bell Jet Ranger helicopter into the hangar when I noticed George standing behind me with his arms folded, as if he were expecting me to make a mistake. And who was I to disappoint him? Even though I was working as slowly and carefully as possible, probably over-trying, my oily sneakers slipped off the clutch, and I almost plunged the tail rotor of the chopper into the back wall of the hangar. I slammed on the brakes, just in time, but when I turned around I saw George shaking his head as if to say, "I knew it."

Luckily, a boss who hated me wasn't enough to deter me. However, when six months passed, and the owners gave the first open slot for a copilot to one of their nephews, I quit. The story would end there except for the wonderful universal law that when one door closes, another opens. This door happened to be named "Harvey."

Harvey Hop ran another Learjet charter company called Hop a Jet, which also is in Fort Lauderdale. He was well over seventy years old, and about six foot five without even an ounce of body fat. More importantly, he was a goodhearted man known for letting newbies fly with him as copilots on charter flights. He did, however, have extremely high expectations of them. When you flew with Harvey, you were also required to sweep and wax his hangar floor, keep the airplane immaculate, make sure the bar on board the plane was stocked and catered, and have the airplane fueled with exactly the right amount for the trip. Furthermore, when Harvey arrived at the airplane, he wanted you to have the right engine running. If you could follow all those rules, you were gold to him.

One day, I approached Harvey and asked if I could fly a trip with him. All he said was, "Leave me your resume, and we'll see." This time I did follow the conventional wisdom that if you pestered people you'd alienate them. I left and made no follow-up calls or visits. To my surprise, he called me about a month later and offered me the chance to fly a charter with him. I was ecstatic. I was also very nervous and wanted to do it perfectly for him.

Harvey and I flew some businessmen to Columbus, Ohio, then returned to Fort Lauderdale, where he unexpectedly asked me if I'd be interested in doing three touch-and-goes in the Lear. Really?! A touch-and-go is a practice maneuver in which a descending plane touches down on the runway but then immediately powers up and takes off again. After the first two, we made a full stop, and he explained that we were going to do a maximum performance climb out—that's when you apply full power while holding the brakes so that when you release the brakes, you virtually launch yourself off the runway. After we rotated off the runway, we immediately leveled off and accelerated to about 300 knots in seconds; then we pulled the nose up to about 25 degrees and climbed like a homesick angel. We crossed the shoreline, which is only about five miles from the airport, at almost 10,000 feet. I remember gasping.

Three things happened to me that day in the Lear. I broke the seemingly impenetrable barrier of getting to fly a jet. I became even more determined to make a career of flying airliners. And I had a very difficult time returning to flight instruction in the Cessna 150. But that one exhilarating flight with Harvey is what led me to aggressively pursue an airline job, which eventually landed me my first break—flying 727s with Iran Air.

Once again, I had learned that persistence and the willingness to delay gratification eventually pay off. You don't need to be somebody's nephew, but you do need to want it, to act on it, and to leave the timing to the universe. In this case, the universe's agenda didn't match my own, and I didn't get a permanent job with Harvey. However, the flight in the Lear helped solidify my goals and added to my piloting experience, something that would never have happened had I not put one foot in front of the other and walked into that airport to make it happen.

During this same period when I was flight instructing, I had another opportunity to choose between action and inaction. I noticed, along with a fellow student pilot named Nick, that the company we worked for was failing. I had two choices: watch and wait for it to fail or do something about it. I made the second choice. I approached the owner, Steve, and made him a proposal. If Nick and I could get the company into the black in six months could we have part ownership of the school? "Absolutely," he said, probably relieved to be free of some of the pressure of managing a complex business. I was only twenty years old at the time, but I knew enough to have an attorney draw up a contract stipulating that Nick and I would become 51 percent owners of the flight school if it were making a profit within six months. Then I went into high gear and spent those six months putting posters up all over South Florida.

The company went into the black, and sure enough, Steve lived up to his part of the bargain and gave us 51 percent ownership. I decided that I wanted to handle the affairs of the school that had directly to do with flying. This was acceptable to everyone. Steve was an Eastern Airlines mechanic and was only interested in maintenance, and Nick was interested in the business end of the school.

About five or six months later, however, I realized there were debts in the company that hadn't been disclosed. I knew that would force it either into receivership or bankruptcy, in spite of my efforts. This deceit could have derailed my career completely, but I came up with another plan. I approached a friend who was a flight instructor at the school and asked him in confidence to put me through all my flying ratings as fast as we could, before the school closed. He agreed, and in essence, I earned all my flight ratings through sweat equity in under a year, thus putting myself in a position to move on and upward.

The bottom line for me is that success relies less on luck and far more on our willingness to act, even if those actions are uncomfortable, maybe even a little out of character. Wanting is not enough; hoping is not enough. Sometimes acting isn't enough either, but when it isn't, it usually leads us somewhere—maybe not to ownership of a company, but to ownership of flight ratings way before we expected to have them.

Cort Aviation promotional poster (Scott Kaye is on the left)

CHAPTER SIX

ENGINE FIRE AT ONE OF THE WORLD'S SCARIEST AIRPORTS

Flying into La Aurora International Airport in Guatemala City can be a scary ride. To start with, the runway itself is an anomaly. It has a pronounced and lengthy dip, which introduces a very dangerous acceleration followed by a deceleration on the takeoff roll. This affects stopping distance, especially important should it be necessary to abort takeoff, and it also increases landing distance because we must accelerate after landing just as we're riding the downhill part. And there's more. At each end of the runway, there's a cliff with a two-thousand-foot drop. Before even getting to that runway, pilots have to weave through tricky mountainous terrain that includes active volcanoes. And did I mention that the altitude of the airport is about a mile, which reduces airplane performance significantly? In short, La Aurora is a pilot's nightmare. It's also alarming to passengers who are looking out their windows at towering mountains surrounding the plane.

The runway in Guatemala is 9,800 feet long and 200 feet wide, but if you land where and how you're supposed to, meaning not too low, you have only about 8,800 feet of runway available. That's not a lot of margin for error, especially when you know that since the runway is bowed and sloped, you can experience illusions about speed and distance and make maneuvers that eat up precious concrete. Those illusions start at only 2,200 feet down the runway, with 6,500 feet of runway beyond that. To simplify, it's possible to go over the cliff at the end of the runway. This has happened more than once. To make it worse, if you have to miss the approach and perform a go-around, the airplane performs worse than if it were at sea level, and all the while there are those mountains right in your face. It's ugly. And it's one of the experiences through which I developed my concentration skills.

Although La Aurora is a challenge for pilots, it's also very exciting, chiefly because most pilots thrive on challenges. And we know, as passengers should know, that we've been highly trained to deal with every one of these complications.

Still, with all its drawbacks, La Aurora logs in at only number seventeen on the list of the twenty-five airports in the world that pilots consider the riskiest. The airport that takes the honors for being the number one scariest is Lukla Tensing-Hillary Airport in Nepal, the same one trekkers must fly into before beginning their climb up Everest. Lukla Tensing-Hillary is a small airport, and it sits at more than 9,500 feet in elevation. Because of that elevation, aircraft can't run on full power. In addition, the runway has a huge mountain on one end and a drop of nearly 3,300 feet on the other end.

At neither of these airports does a pilot have a wide margin of error given the tremendously adverse conditions. That became abundantly clear to me one day at La Aurora when I was attempting a takeoff in a

757, and things suddenly went very wrong.

After four years as a 727 flight engineer, three years as a 727 first officer, fourteen months as a 747 first officer, and five years as a 737 captain, I had finally arrived at the 757 aircraft, which I'd had my eye on for many years. In my opinion, the 757 is the sexiest looking jet airliner made. It's a Boeing, so that makes it a superior airplane right off the bat. The beauty of this plane lies in its extreme length from nose to tail, with the landing gear positioned far enough back so it doesn't mar the sleekness of the forward half of the fuselage. Additionally, the two engines are so large compared to the narrowness of the fuselage that it gives the appearance of extreme power. Not only is it beautiful, but it's extremely fun to fly, very responsive and easy to handle, and with a long range for its size. I view the 757 as the Ferrari of the aviation world.

757—sleek and sexy

Having said all that, it's still a piece of machinery that requires maintenance. A machine as complex as a commercial jet has so many parts that sometimes even a sharp, highly trained maintenance person can overlook something small when disassembling and reassembling the plane's components. One day I was the recipient of one of these small oversights on a 757 as I was taking off from Guatemala City, a small slip that caused me a monumental problem.

On that day, we were lined up in the takeoff position on Runway 01, and the tower had given us clearance to proceed. I applied the power, and the airplane began to accelerate—a little more slowly than normal, but that was to be expected given the high elevation. If I recall correctly, the V1 speed (the "go" or "no-go" decision point for continuing or aborting the takeoff) was 140 knots. Above that speed, if you abort the takeoff, there won't be enough runway left to stop. The general theory is that it's better to continue at that point and take the problem or malfunction with you into the air and deal with it later.

The plane had reached about 130 knots when an engine fire bell sounded in the cockpit. Since I was below V1, (the go/no-go decision speed) I aborted the takeoff. A fire bell is one of five events that would justify an aborted takeoff below V1. The other four are:

- A predictive wind shear warning (PWS)
- A directional control problem (usually from an engine failure)
- Any warning light that flashes red
- Anything a captain personally deems dangerous should the plane become airborne

We trained for these emergencies over and over again in the simulator so that our responses became automatic and built into our muscle memory. This is intentional because there is no time to process the information and make a decision when the problem occurs. It's why pilots are not thinking in terms of takeoff during a takeoff roll, but rather in terms of an abort, in case that should suddenly become necessary.

If the copilot is making the takeoff, it's protocol for the captain to take control of the airplane and execute the abort. That day, I was making the takeoff. The procedure for an abort is:

- Pull the throttles back
- Raise the speed brake levers
- Wait for the airplane to come to a complete stop on maximum auto brakes

Braking is handled mostly by technology. The auto brake system has a setting called RTO (rejected takeoff). It applies harder pressure to the brakes than any human being is capable of applying. To protect pilots against the lunge forward during braking, they wear not just seatbelts but shoulder harnesses, one over each shoulder. Just as in a car, if forward pressure is exerted on the harnesses, they lock up.

As I braked during the aborted takeoff that day, I was surprised when I lunged forward with much more force than I was expecting, force that far exceeded the mock-up of such a high-speed abort in the simulators. All I could see at that split second was the end of the runway coming up frighteningly fast, followed by a two-thousand-foot straight drop. I was scared out of my wits on one level but managed to remain cool on another, immersed in the moment, and fully focused on stopping. Time went into slow motion. After the airplane came to a complete stop, it was rocking back and forth like a van filled with rambunctious teenagers. Now I had to turn my attention to the fire.

Besides the fire bell, many other signals in the cockpit warn of an engine or cargo-pit fire. One of them is an engine "fire handle," which lights up red during a fire. To extinguish the fire, a crew member pulls the fire handle and then rotates it, which closes all the valves in the airplane that allow any air, fluid, or fuel into the engine. When the handle is rotated, one of two Freon bottles is discharged into the engine to extinguish the fire. If the first bottle doesn't put the fire out, the handle is rotated in the opposite direction to release the second bottle. In this case, it took both bottles to get the fire out. To make matters worse, the intense heat generated by the emergency stop caused the brakes to catch fire. There is a fire department at the airport, and luckily, I speak Spanish. I was able to quickly advise that I needed a fire truck to come out and spray my brakes.

After we ran all of our checklists, my copilot turned to me, showed me that his hands were shaking, and asked if mine were shaking as well. They weren't, but only because I was directly involved in getting the airplane stopped, and I was so focused I didn't have time to process anything else. Yes, I had been scared seeing the end of the runway approach, but like being in a car and watching as someone is about to T-bone you, all I could do was brace myself.

The airplane wasn't about to go anywhere. I called for a tow tractor to bring it to the gate, where maintenance proceeded to remove the engine to ship it back to San Francisco for a rebuild. We booked into a hotel, went out to dinner, and rehashed the whole incident over wine.

In the end, it turned out that a maintenance oversight caused the engine fire. Someone had installed one of the fuel line nuts to the corresponding bolt backward. The plane had been flown in that condition for three months, and all the while the nut was slowly being vibrated loose. Finally, it was fully stripped and gave way, just as I was making that takeoff. Raw fuel poured out of that line to the outside casing of the engine igniting a fire . . . and believe me, it was a big fire.

I understood how this mistake could have happened because it's difficult to discern the correct end of a nut. But attention to detail is crucial when it comes to work where risk is involved. Although it's easy when doing mechanical work all day to get into a sort of mindless rhythm, if one is truly focused on the "now," such oversights don't happen. Of course, I'm happy that we didn't shoot past the end of the runway and plummet two thousand feet. But the experience remains in my psyche, and to this day, I shudder when I think about it. Still, it served me well. Whenever I'm entering a high-risk situation, I give due thought to the possible unintended consequences and how to react to them. And I like to think that there's a maintenance worker out there somewhere who's given due thought to the fact that all it takes to bring down a 220,000-pound, eighty-million-dollar jet is one little backward nut.

CHAPTER SEVEN

The Strike that Led to a Homer

In 1985, after thirteen years of laying the groundwork for that elusive major airline job, I was called for interviews by four different airlines in one month—Delta, Northwest, American, and United. I was elated when United offered me an interview; it had bases on the West Coast, my home coast, and it was one of the few airlines with a fleet of 747s. It had something else going on too, something I wasn't aware of, that affected the next thirty years of my life—a labor dispute between management and the pilots union. Not yet knowing that, I began to prepare for my interview.

A company in business at that time called FAPA (Future Airline Pilots of America) published a newsletter targeting pilots who aspired to get hired by a major airline. The publication provided details about interview questions, psychological test materials, and other valuable information. In the case of United, the interview process was four days long, including two separate visits to Denver.

The first two-day session consisted of a very stringent physical exam. The need for eyeglasses would immediately disqualify you. The exam was nerve-racking, and I found myself asking, "What are the odds of me clearing all these hurdles?" United also administered many psychological tests, among them the MMPI (Minneapolis Multiphasic Personality Inventory), an extremely long exam that measures personality traits and psychopathology, and which I had "practiced" for earlier. It involves several hundred questions, and unless you know what will be asked and are prepared to answer with complete honesty, it is impossible to pass.

Another test was a cognitive recognition test in which they flashed onto a screen a card with numbers appearing in different colors. They flashed the cards so quickly there was barely enough time to process the images. In the first phase, they asked me to just state the number. In the next phase, they wanted me to state the color of the ink in which the number was printed. Having done my homework with FAPA, I learned how to blur my eyes during the second phase so that I couldn't really see the number and the color alone stood out.

There were several other tests that I can't recall, but I do remember they were challenging and included math, aptitude, and memory tests. I also remember that I didn't see anything during those tests that I hadn't seen during my preparation. That was a relief—no surprises. Still, by the time I finished on the first day, I was as drained as I can ever remember.

The next day, they administered the remaining tests and gave us a United Airlines orientation session. Later that day, they sent all the applicants home, saying, "We'll let you know. We'll contact you." It was very impersonal.

After about a month of waiting on pins and needles, I received a letter inviting me back for the next phase, which consisted of interviews and a simulator evaluation. Again, I was well prepared by FAPA and knew what to expect.

At that time, I was flying as a Boeing 737 captain for People Express Airlines based in New Jersey. The United simulator was based on a Boeing 767, which is really a 737 on steroids. They evaluated my flying skills, and then gave me an engine fire with a loud fire bell that couldn't be silenced. They wanted to see how I would handle flying a plane while distracted. When I came out of the simulator, I felt like I had nailed it, rather like a comedian who walks off stage with his audience rolling on the floor in laughter. I was right. The evaluator later told me it was one of the best performances he'd seen in weeks.

Next was the first interview, and by then I knew things at United weren't what they seemed. I had discovered that the company was creating a pool of 570 pilots, known as "The 570," to work during a pilot strike expected to begin on May 17, 1985, if no labor agreement had been reached. I was in that group of 570, and when I found out, I realized I was trapped.

This shadow made the atmosphere during the interview tense. It got off to a bad start even before the subject of the strike was raised. When I arrived, I had reached out to shake the hand of my interviewer, and he had quickly withdrawn his hand with the comment that a handshake wasn't necessary. I found that a little strange, but soon understood when I noticed he had what appeared to be some sort of nerve damage in his hand and couldn't straighten his fingers. Soon, the issue of the potential strike came up. He told me that if I wasn't willing to work during a strike, then I might as well leave and consider myself no longer a candidate for employment. In fact, I was asked directly if I intended to strike or scab. I said I intended to work. All of this seemed highly immoral and illegal to me, rather like extortion, but what was I to do? I was infuriated but simply prayed that an agreement would be reached before I had to make a decision that would probably end my airline career.

Because of the stress of the interview, compounded by the fact that I knew I was being scrutinized for whether I would strike or scab, I forgot at the end about the interviewer's damaged hand and once again went to shake it. "UH OH! I really screwed this up," I thought. Later I found out that they were so desperate for pilots to work during the strike that I probably could've picked up a paperweight from his desk, thrown it through his office window, and still been hired. And I was hired . . . and soon fired.

I was in the United simulator building being trained when I was called out to answer a call in the phone bank in the outside hallway. On the other end of the line was a United flight manager in Chicago who asked me point blank if I intended to work on May 17. The Air Line Pilots Association (ALPA), the pilots union, had advised us to tell management "yes" because there was as yet no strike and a "no" would have ended our jobs right then and there. The flight manager told me that much on the phone. He said that if I was going to answer that question in the negative, then I should proceed back to the hotel, pack my suitcase and return home. Again, I crossed my fingers that an agreement between the pilots and United would be reached in time. But it was not to be.

On May 17, the strike officially began, and we, "The 570," signed in at the picket line, returned home, and refused to work during a strike. Retaliation was swift. The CEO unilaterally fired all 570 of us. Fortunately, I was able to retain my job as a 737 captain at People

Express in New Jersey. But when the strike ended after twenty-nine days, United hired a new group of 539 pilots, known as "The 539," to replace us. Thus began the legal war.

After one year and several court battles that ALPA waged against United on behalf of The 570, a judge ordered the CEO to rehire every one of us, ruling that it was illegal to fire us for refusing to work during a strike. So far, so good. However, there was now the issue of which pilot group had seniority—my original group of 570 or the subsequent group of 539 hired after the strike began. According to management, it was The 539. ALPA disagreed. It maintained that since The 570 members were on the property and in training before The 539, we held seniority. Job progression in the aviation industry is based on seniority, so this was a critical issue for career advancement. We spent years slugging it out in court, all through the anti-labor climate of the 1980s and into the 1990s, when we lost every single legal battle. Finally, in 1992, we made it to the United States Supreme Court, which ruled in our favor stating that United had breached its promise to The 570 to have their seniority based upon their initial training dates rather than their recall date a year after they were fired. The company was forced to reinstate our original seniority. It was a long wait, but when the decision finally came in, I was immediately senior enough to bid for a captain's position at United on the 737. Something else came out of it too—a two-dollar specially engraved dog tag purchased at a military supply store that I wear to this day.

My anger at the airline management, the CEO, and the greed and selfishness of industry tycoons was out of control during these years. I knew this anger was a direct throwback to the childhood rejection I experienced with my father and to the powerlessness I felt then. But knowing this didn't help. I can't even guess how many gallons of cortisol pumped through my body during that first year of the strike and its aftermath, but I knew even then it couldn't have been good for my health. I wanted to be healthy. I had big plans in life. So I made the decision to learn to control my anger.

As a token of that commitment, I bought a stainless steel dog tag, and took it to a trophy engraving shop where I had the following well-known prayer engraved on it: "God grant me the serenity to accept the things I cannot change; courage to change the things I can; and wisdom to know the difference." Now, and for all the years since, whenever I feel rage coming on, I clutch that dog tag, and it instantly calms me down. It's my own personal anger-control technique, with about a 90 percent success rate. I may have lost a lot of time and money thanks to the repercussions of that strike, but what I gained can't be measured by either.

A few years ago, while doing some training in Denver, I passed the wall where I'd taken the phone call in 1985 from the United flight manager demanding to know whether I intended to work through the strike. There were no longer any phone booths on that wall, just the marks of the drywall repair that was done when the phones were removed. I asked my first officer to take a picture of me standing by that very spot, almost thirty years later, a man who had gambled his career on a principle, and who was now a veteran pilot.

CHAPTER EIGHT

Gratitude – The Key to a Smooth Landing

After being reintegrated back into the company, it immediately became clear that there was a tremendous amount of hostility between my group, The 570, returning a year after being fired for honoring the strike, and the other group, The 539, which had been hired to replace us. By virtue of our recall, the replacement group had advanced from FE (flight engineer) positions to those of first officers, also known as copilots. Flight engineer (also called "plumber") is a nonflying position, meaning the FE doesn't manipulate the flight controls as the captain and first officer do. When asked what airplane they were on and their role, ("which seat and fleet?"), flight engineers would say "I sit sideways," or "back seat," or "I plumb." An FO would say "I face forward," or "the right seat," which would mean they're piloting. A captain would just say that he's captain, or sometimes "the left seat," but never, "I face forward." That's implied.

Besides my resentment over the advancement of The 539, one of the consequences of the strike and new contract with United management was establishment of a two-tier pay scale. Any new pilot hired after ratification of the new pilot contract would be at a lower pay scale for five years, known to us as "B Scale." My pay was about 60 percent lower than that of an "A Scale" pilot in the same position. Let the cortisol flow.

I remember a trip to La Guardia Airport in New York when I was serving as FE on a Boeing 727, aka "the three holer" because it has three rear-mounted engines and their inlets at the front of the plane look simply like holes. All planes have such nicknames. The 737 is known as "the guppy." The 747 is called "the whale." And the 757 is likened to a "sensuous woman" because the fuselage is long, sleek, and narrow, which makes the gear struts look like long legs. In addition, the two wing-mounted engines look especially large, in contrast to the streamlined fuselage (use your imagination on that one).

At that time, the 727 still had flight engineer panels, something commercial airliners have since replaced with an overhead panel that pilots control, thus rendering the flight engineer position obsolete. All of today's airliners are designed and built that way. In addition to sitting at the FE panel, plumbers were responsible for everything related to the aircraft's performance in the event of a malfunction or "deferred" piece of equipment, a defective piece that's not critical for flight and will receive maintenance at the next opportunity. We had to be intimately familiar with all the aircraft systems, which is why we were considered to be "plumbing" until we were senior enough to bid for a first officer position. It's a busy and demanding job, but an entry-level position we all had to endure until we made "the right seat."

While preparing for takeoff that day, I was in the middle of a complicated performance problem and was buried under charts and graphs scattered on the FE table, a work surface at the bottom of the FE panel. The first officer, who was one of The 539 who had replaced us a year earlier and on the higher "A Scale," put his arm on the back of his chair and drawled, "Man, I sure could use a cup of coffee." The first officer on a Boeing 727 has very little to do while the aircraft is sitting at the gate, which is why we had a standing joke back then: "Window Heat, Pitot Heat, What's To Eat?" Pitot tubes provide air pressure to several of the instruments in the cockpit, and it's the first officer's job to make sure they're heated enough to prevent ice buildup, which he does by turning on two switches. His only other significant task is to turn on two other switches that heat the windscreen (the windshield on a jet), thus rendering it shatterproof should there be a bird strike on takeoff, and/or a climb-out at high speed. I suppressed my anger for that ill-timed mandate for coffee, and instead replied, "That sounds like a great idea. As long as you're up, would you mind getting me a Diet Coke?" He was infuriated. I then told him as calmly as possible that I was very busy, and it had been inconsiderate of him to expect me to run an errand for him. The captain interjected with a cavalier, "All right boys, let's all get along," and I put it all out of my mind and proceeded with my work . . . but without a Diet Coke.

Sitting in the cockpit with my charts and no soft drink, I began to turn to other work environments. I could have been working at McDonald's or as a greeter at Walmart or not even working at all—and instead I was in the cockpit of a 727 airliner. That thought alone was enough to ease the fury and make me appreciate what I had, no matter how frustrating the circumstances. With that one shift in thought, I quickly came back down to earth, figuratively speaking, and got on with it. Nowadays, I apply the same thinking to life outside the cockpit. "How could things be worse?" "What do I need to feel grateful for?"

CHAPTER NINE

FIVE AIRPLANE CRASHES – ONE PILOT'S POINT OF VIEW

CRASH #1: UNITED FLIGHT 585 IN COLORADO SPRINGS

In the dreary roll call of aviation accidents, some plane crashes seem especially significant, either because of the changes they inspired in procedure or equipment, the mystery that surrounds them, or the lessons they teach about human or technological behavior. Five of these come to mind, two of which involved United Airlines and three of which didn't, all of which are still in our collective professional consciousness.

The first is the 1991 crash of UAL 585, a United Airlines Boeing 737 that was landing in Colorado Springs. Warnings about this crash occurred in the week before it happened. The first occurred during a flight when the plane's rudder inexplicably deflected to the right, an event known as "hard-over." The problem disappeared when the pilots switched off the yaw damper, a device that automatically commands small rudder adjustments during flight. Mechanics then replaced a part called the yaw-damper coupler and returned the plane to service.

Two days later, a different flight crew reported that the rudder again moved off to the right; the new coupler had evidently made no difference. This time mechanics replaced a valve in the yaw damper and again returned the plane to service.

Four days after that, another crew wasn't as lucky. As they were bringing the same airplane down for a routine landing in Colorado Springs, the jet suddenly flipped to the right at one thousand feet above the ground and dived straight down, smashing into a city park and killing all twenty-five on board. The tower controller reported that the plane "looked like a dropped pencil going straight down."

I was familiar with the captain of the plane, Harold Green, although I'd never met him. But I can say emphatically that he made it to captain at United Airlines and flew passenger jets only because he had proved his ability and bested whatever an unforgiving training department could throw at him, just like the rest of us. A meteorological force that was not fully understood at the time caused this crash, although investigators focused primarily on a mechanical problem.

It soon came to light that an uncommanded erroneous rudder movement may have forced the plane into what is known as a "split S." This maneuver is used during air combat to quickly disengage from an opponent. The pilot half-rolls his aircraft to an inverted position and executes a descending half-loop, resulting in level flight in the opposite direction and at a lower altitude.

After the crash, investigators dismantled the rudder power control unit

(PCU), which is a series of valves and linkages that connect the pilot's rudder input or yaw damper input into the movement of the rudder itself. They noted a white, powdery substance on the internal components of the yaw damper, and tiny drops of water and chips of bronze in some PCU cavities.

In the PCU, there's a dual servo valve, which consists of a cylindrical metal slide about the size of a cigarette, which is positioned inside a slightly larger slide. The servo slides work together to direct the proper flow of pressurized hydraulic fluid used to move the rudder. It's crucial to keep even minute debris out of the servo valve because the spaces separating the slides from each other and from their housing wall are no more than five microns, a gap invisible to the human eye. Contaminants could jam the slides or clog a valve opening, sending hydraulic fluid flowing in the wrong sequence and inadvertently moving the rudder.

The investigators found that the servo's slides were severely jammed and pounded them apart with a hammer. They discovered that three servo-valve parts were missing: a spring, spring guide, and end cap. These three missing parts prevent the outer slide from moving too far within the housing.

The servo valve on the doomed 737 had failed to transfer fluid and maintain pressure according to specifications. However, the investigators agreed it was working well enough, and concluded there was no evidence that the valve contributed to the crash. What then did cause this crash?

Boeing suggested that a freak gust of wind, which it called a "sideways swirling wind rotor," bounced like a horizontal tornado off the Rocky Mountain foothills and flipped the 737 into a "split S" dive.

Some investigators expressed doubt about Boeing's theory, saying it would take incredible strength for wind to pull a thirty-eight-ton airplane into a split S dive. For Boeing's theory to make sense, the rotor wind would have had to hit the aircraft head on and then turned earthward at just the right moment to drive the plane into the ground. Nothing in aviation history suggested such a phenomenon was possible. The focus shifted back to the rudder PCU, with no immediate resolution.

About a year and a half after the crash, another captain was performing his pre-takeoff check at O'Hare International and didn't like the way his 737 rudder pedals were behaving. The right pedal seemed stiffer than usual, and he could only push the left one about a quarter of the way to the floor.

United removed the PCU from the jet, ferried it to the airline's maintenance center in San Francisco, and began experimenting with it. There, sources say, a mechanic discovered that he could trigger a specific kind of rudder malfunction, called a reversal, by putting the spring, spring guide, and end cap slightly out of adjustment. He established that a PCU could receive a command to move the rudder left and erroneously move the rudder full right. Such a reversal could happen if the spring, spring guide, and end cap were not in the precise alignment needed to prevent the outer slide from moving too far.

Three years after the crash, in March 1994, the FAA ordered airlines to replace all three parts in all 737 PCUs. I vividly remember when this was unfolding. You can bet that I was performing my control checks on the ground, especially the rudder pedals, with great vigor.

As with any plane crash, something positive always results. In this case, besides the discoveries about the PCUs, investigators conducted an in-depth study of the behavior of wind flow around peaks and through mountain passes that yielded valuable information. The National Transportation Safety Board recommended that the FAA develop a program to address the hazards of the meteorology in and around mountainous terrain. At United, we developed a full program known as controlled flight into terrain (CFIT). There is, as it turns out, enough power in some of these thermals and rotors to bring an airplane down (interestingly enough, it's sailplane pilots who know more about these weather phenomena than professional meteorologists). As a result, we underwent extensive CFIT training in the simulator and an airplane. Another benefit from the investigation into this crash was the development of enhanced predictive wind shear systems onboard airplanes.

In the final analysis of UAL 585, it was concluded that the wiring to the solenoid of the PCU was loose and as a result, it gave an uncommanded rudder displacement. As a point of interest, it was also reported that the day after the accident, there was severe wind shear in the vicinity. The final, official, probable cause of the UAL 585 crash was rudder-system malfunction. It was determined ten years after the accident.

In my opinion as a pilot, both the PCU and the weather combined to cause this crash. The malfunctioning PCU was a factor, but the extremely powerful winds coming off the mountains exacerbated the situation and pinned the captain into a position without sufficient rudder authority to recover.

Knowing these potential hidden dangers, I wouldn't allow an air traffic controller to give me a descent clearance around peaks and mountain passes that brought me too low too soon, simply to accommodate his desire to flow air traffic around me into an airport arrival corridor. I knew these controllers considered me a pain in the butt, but I had to remind myself that I was the one carrying passengers in a plane, while the controller was sitting in a comfortable room safely on the ground. Controllers are there for pilots and not the other way around and all I had to say to quiet them was, "Request maintain higher altitude." They knew exactly why.

This accident, like some others, reminded me yet again that I'm in a profession that has a high element of risk. Even though flying is statistically safer than automobile travel, in some ways, you have more control and more escape routes when driving a car. Imagine driving along the freeway, and the steering wheel pulls suddenly full left toward a concrete median barrier. When this happens, your initial instinct is probably to "death grip" the steering wheel and hit the brakes to prevent an impact. I couldn't do that in an airborne plane. In a car, you'll also probably quickly assess your speed and choose the best angle for impact to minimize your chance of injury, something else pilots can't do. What pilots do have on their side though, is training.

There are so many moving parts in an airplane, like the rudder system in Flight 585, that when something goes wrong, it generally comes at you like a curveball. Sudden or not, at that point, you're stuck with it, and you'd better have the ability to quickly put together a game plan. United addresses this challenge in training. They throw something at pilots that is absolutely unexpected, just to observe how they handle it. By collecting data on these results, they can then fine-tune the program and prepare pilots to handle emergencies, or at least the ones we can imagine.

CRASH #2: UNITED FLIGHT 232 IN SIOUX CITY, IOWA

About an hour after takeoff, the crew of United Flight 232, a DC-10 en route from Denver to Chicago in July 1989, heard and felt a loud bang while the plane was over Iowa. The pilots determined by visual, aural, and instrument indications the aircraft had lost the center engine and ran the checklists that involve shutting down the engine—no big deal as they had two good remaining engines. In a DC-10, the center engine is mounted on the tail of the aircraft while the other two engines are wing mounted.

During the checklist, crew members noticed they were losing pressure in three hydraulic systems as well as hydraulic fluid quantity. The aircraft went into an uncommanded slight right turn. They disconnected the autopilot but found they couldn't control the airplane manually. They pulled the power back on the left engine, which discontinued the right turn and brought the wings back to a level state. Soon, however, the aircraft slowly began to bank into a right turn again, and the crew declared an emergency. Minneapolis traffic control gave them a vector toward Sioux City, Iowa, which has a nine-thousand-foot runway.

At this point, the crew had no control over any of the airplane flight control surfaces. The only way to control the direction of the plane was by using asymmetrical power between the left and right engines. A deadheading United crewmember happened to be onboard, and he was allowed into the cockpit to help with the constant changing of power between the left and right engines to keep the plane under as much control as possible. While the plane was descending, it made two slow complete 360-degree right turns.

At nine thousand feet and about twenty-one miles from the airport, air traffic control directed the airplane south of the airport to keep it east of the city and to set up for an approach to a runway landing toward the northwest. In the interim, one of the flight attendants called the cockpit and said he noticed damage to the horizontal stabilizer, which is on the tail and controls the up-and-down pitch of the airplane. Meanwhile, despite all his efforts, the deadheading crewmember who was controlling the throttles could no longer overcome the airplane's tendency to continue a right turn.

Miraculously, with the airport straight ahead of them at twelve miles, the airplane ceased turning right, and the crew found themselves lined up for runway 22, which is 6,600 feet long. In my opinion, this is inexplicable and smacks of some kind of divine intervention.

The crew had already told the flight attendants to brief the passengers for an emergency landing and was furiously running all of its checklists to make sure nothing was overlooked. It was very busy in that cockpit, and I know something of how that feels. A pilot in those circumstances is more focused on the task at hand than any human being can ever be on any project under normal conditions.

Even though they had the right turn under control, the crew still could not manage the speed of the airplane or its sink rate. I can only imagine how horrifying it must have been to watch the airspeed decrease as the sink rate increased. Flight 232 was descending at 1,600 feet per minute when it should have been descending at about 700 feet per minute. To put things in perspective, its descent rate was almost twenty-seven feet per second—doable for a touch down, but one that would definitely be a hard landing. Of greater concern was the speed. Unable to lower the flaps because there were no hydraulics, the plane touched down at 215 knots when it should have touched down at about 150 knots. At that speed, you eat up runway length in no time at all, careening into parking lots and warehouses. No good can come of a 215-knot landing, and it didn't.

The landing started as well as it could have. Phenomenal airmanship put the plane down right at the beginning of the runway, which is extraordinarily difficult to accomplish at 215 knots. Unfortunately, the right wing touched the concrete of the runway before the landing gear did. Because it was traveling so fast, and its sink rate was so high, the airplane broke up upon impact and exploded into a huge fireball, while cartwheeling down the runway nose over tail.

In spite of all that, 185 people survived the crash, including all four cockpit crew members. I knew of those crew members, and I've met two of them since the accident. Sadly, 111 people did not survive the crash, yet the numbers are still nothing short of amazing. Investigators who conducted simulator tests after the accident that replicated the conditions of the plane and flight were unable to put the airplane on the runway at all. This is a strong testament to the airmanship of the United crew that day, and to its training.

The most important evidence for accident investigators was the fan disk found in a field near the crash site. The disk holds the fan blades at the inlet of the engine, and this disk showed fractures because of metal fatigue. That meant this was a "human error" accident—maintenance workers had failed to spot the fractures before the accident. As a result, the FAA issued airworthiness directives mandating inspections of the fan blades on other DC-10s. All DC-10 operators were required to modify the hydraulic systems by adding enough redundancy to prevent a loss of all hydraulics. Additionally, airlines were required to change the way they conduct engine inspections.

When I reflect upon this accident, it reminds me yet again that one second everything can be fine, as it is 99.9 percent of the time, and then out of nowhere, you're in the 0.1 percent, and something horrific is happening. That's the nature of aviation—hours and hours of boredom, punctuated by moments of sheer terror.

Crash #3: Asiana Flight 214 in San Francisco

Perhaps the most frustrating airline accidents are those that are preventable, as was the case with Asiana 214 from Seoul Korea, which crashed on approach to San Francisco in 2013. Although fatalities were low, it was a significant crash because it involved crew interaction, an issue that seldom gets attention.

The approach of 214, a Boeing 777, started normally. It intercepted the final approach course about fourteen miles from the runway at an altitude slightly above the desired three-degree glide path, which is common for San Francisco due to the use of parallel approaches to two different runways. Controllers use this method of keeping one airplane slightly higher than the other to avoid collisions.

The Korean crew was instructed by air traffic control to maintain 180 knots until five miles from the runway, a higher than normal speed that is typical of San Francisco at certain peak travel times to keep the heavy flow of traffic moving. However, once the pilots were given their clearance, they mismanaged their descent, and the plane was soon well above the desired three-degree glide path. The pilot at the controls, therefore, set up a 1,500-feet-per-minute descent to get back on the glide path.

As the airplane reached five hundred feet above airport elevation, the point at which Asiana's procedures dictate that the approach must be stabilized, the plane was still slightly above the desired glide path. It reached the proper approach speed of 137 knots, but the thrust levers were at idle, which caused the airplane to decelerate rather quickly—1,500 feet per minute when it should have been about 700 hundred feet per minute. What followed was a series of mistakes and miscalculations that soon led to disaster. First, the captain called for "flaps 30," a setting of the movable flight surfaces on the rear of the wings that was incompatible with the high speed the plane was traveling. Next, in an attempt to increase the airplane's descent rate and capture the desired glide path, he selected an autopilot mode called FLCH SPD (flight level change speed). This initiated a climb to 3,000 feet, for which the autopilot had been previously set. In making this decision, the pilot showed he didn't understand the autopilot system and how it integrates with other operations. Both pilots were taken by surprise when the plane began to climb. At this point, a pilot should disconnect the autopilot and try to recapture the glide path manually. It's always faster to maneuver an airplane manually because there's a lag built into the autopilot. The Asiana captain did disconnect the autopilot, but tremendous drag was created because the plane was still at idle thrust and had all those flaps and the landing gear hanging out, which caused the airplane to decelerate further. Worst of all, he did that too near the ground, demonstrating a lack of basic flying skills. This caused the autopilot to change to hold mode, which no longer allows the autothrottles to control the airspeed, yet another reflection of the crew's lack of understanding. Neither the pilot at the controls, the pilot monitoring, nor the observer in the cockpit noted this change to the "HOLD" mode.

About 1.4 miles from the runway the airplane continued to descend at 1,500 feet per minute; now it was traveling *below* the glide path and below the target approach speed. The pilot pulled back on the controls in an attempt to regain the glide path, which further slowed the airplane. This move is comparable to driving a car uphill without stepping on the gas pedal until the car comes to a stop; the equivalent of an aerodynamic stall in an airplane. He was already at the point where it was unsalvageable without an immediate blast of thrust, and I mean firewalling it to full thrust and executing a go-around maneuver, which is standard procedure at United.

By this time, it was clear that Flight 214 was seriously destabilized, but the pilots continued their approach. Too slow, too low, and on the verge of a stall is a lethal cocktail of circumstances in an airplane. By 200 feet, the flight crew became aware of the low airspeed and low glide path conditions but, incredibly, still didn't initiate a go-around. Finally, when the plane was below 100 feet and the pilots heard a loud ground proximity warning alert, the copilot shoved the throttle levers as far forward as possible, a move that pilots call cobbing the power, and called for a go-around. Too late! At that point such a maneuver is impossible; the plane no longer has the necessary performance capability to remain airborne.

One of the probable reasons for the tardy decision to abort this flight is that many pilots have an aversion to performing a go-around, as research has proved. This was not true at United, however. We had a very specific set of guidelines that constitute a "stabilized approach," and if any of those guidelines aren't met, a go-around is mandatory.

Because of my training, I would never have gotten myself into Flight 214's position. But if I somehow did, I can only imagine that there would be nothing left to do but say, "Please God, get me out of this!"

Kaboom! Asiana hit the seawall prior to the runway.

Knowing what I know about the lag response to cobbing the power, there must have been a feeling of utter helplessness when they finally did it and the plane didn't immediately respond. That would be similar to seeing your car headed for a telephone pole, slamming your steering wheel full left to avoid it, and finding that the car doesn't respond.

After the airplane hit the wall, the tail broke off. The plane then slid along the runway, lifted partially into the air, spun around, and impacted the ground a final time. The force of the impact inflated two escape slides within the cabin, injuring and temporarily trapping two flight attendants. Six occupants were ejected from the airplane, three fatally. Two firefighting vehicles later rolled over one of the ejected passengers. Two of those ejected weren't wearing seatbelts; if they had been, they would likely have remained in the cabin and survived.

Once the airplane came to a stop, the now separated right engine caught fire, so one of the flight attendants initiated an evacuation. Ninety-eight percent of the passengers successfully self-evacuated, and firefighters extricated five passengers who were injured. One of them later died.

The flight crew's insufficient monitoring of airspeed indications during the approach was the result of erroneous expectations, increased workload, fatigue, and automation reliance. These are all areas in which we received extensive training at United, and I do mean extensive. In addition, the Asiana accident supports my fear that we're now into a generation of pilots who grew up on video games and never flew analog instrumentation in their early training. They therefore lack certain skills to fall back on during an emergency, skills that older pilots developed during their early training.

In the Asiana crash, technical skills and understanding were inadequate, and so was confidence. After the accident, the trainee captain who was piloting Asiana 214 told investigators he was stressed about the approach to the unfamiliar airport. He found the approach difficult to perform with such a large plane and without the electronic system that tracks a plane's glide path, which was down for maintenance. He also demonstrated a lack of understanding of the autothrottle, saying it "always maintains speed" so he "didn't think about that." At United, we were expected to monitor cockpit equipment throughout a flight, even when the autopilot was engaged. And in this case, the autothrottle wasn't even engaged; the pilot simply presumed it was. The trainee pilot also told investigators, with refreshing candor, that he felt unprepared for this landing because he hadn't studied his training information hard enough.

Three passengers died in the Asiana crash, and more than 200 were sent to hospitals. It's not difficult to see how several elements came together before this unhappy outcome at the approach end of Runway 28R. But there was another factor in this accident, one not mentioned in the accident report, and that's the cultural factor.

In many Asian cultures it's not acceptable to challenge authority, and in the case of the Asiana flight, this custom allowed many elemental errors to unfold unchallenged. Had it been acceptable, this landing could have been salvaged much earlier than five miles from the runway. There is evidence that the crew onboard noticed the problems emerging but hesitated to interfere. For example, no one suggested a timely switch to manual control of the plane because this would have challenged the pilot's authority.

Through studies of cockpit voice recorders and flight data recorders, investigators have learned that fatal accidents are the culmination of six or seven factors that lead to a tragic outcome, and often, as in the case of Asiana, one of these factors is the failure of crew members to assert themselves when problems arise. Although the crew of Flight 214 did eventually react, the official report is that they did too little and too late.

At United, crew member communication has been incorporated into the training syllabus for well over twenty-five years. It emphasizes the need to speak up when you see anything that doesn't look quite right, regardless of whether you're a captain or first officer. There is so much emphasis on asserting oneself, that I've seen people perform spectacularly in the simulator as far as technical skills go and still be reprimanded for not speaking up when things were going wrong.

It seems to me that many of life's disasters happen in the same way as the Asiana accident—a half dozen things go wrong before the disaster itself, and all are warnings and opportunities to true our course. We should be able to avert personal disasters by recognizing those errors as they're happening, then doing things differently before we go bankrupt, get a divorce, or die prematurely. To me, that's what taking action sooner rather than later is truly about, even if it means challenging authority.

Something I learned very early on when I transitioned to "glass cockpits," the term pilots use for a flight deck with digitized instrument readouts completely integrated with the plane's computers and autopilot, is that whenever a crew finds itself asking "What the hell is this thing doing?" that's the time to disconnect everything and just, as we said at United, *fly the airplane.* I now find this to be a metaphor for all the curveballs life can throw. Whenever I'm hit by one, I can more easily recognize those half a dozen things that led up to it. Not all can be avoided, but there are times when if you listen to your inner self early in the sequence, you can prevent the snowballing effect. Or maybe I should call it the seawalling effect.

CRASH #4: MALAYSIA FLIGHT 370 OVER THE INDIAN OCEAN

Although an explanation is found for almost all airplane crashes, a few will always remain an enigma. Malaysia Airlines Flight 370, which was en route from Kuala Lumpur to Beijing, may be one of them. However, I believe that somewhere, someone knows what happened to that plane March 8, 2014, but isn't talking. I don't know why, maybe it's to save face, but the silence and mystery have led to many conspiracy theories, some of them logical, some of them fantastical.

Complicating the mystery around Flight 370 is the communications data, much of it supplied by Inmarsat, a British satellite communications company.

Once Flight 370 went missing, an Inmarsat ground station in Perth, Australia, checked the logs and discovered that while the Boeing 777's communications systems were switched off, the plane and the satellite kept saying "hello" to each other every hour. "Having messages for six hours after the plane is lost is probably the biggest disbelief."

Malaysian authorities confirmed that a communications system known as ACARS (Aircraft Communications Addressing and Reporting System) was turned off, according to a March 18, 2014, article in The Washington Post. Reporter Brian Fung wrote that the part of the system that automatically communicates with ground stations was disabled, but the plane's equipment continued to respond to "pings"

(sometimes called digital "handshakes") from a satellite. Turning that off would have required access to equipment buried in the electronics bay deep in the aircraft's belly, which is obviously out of reach of pilots during flight.

Analyzing the discrepancy of satellite frequency known as the Doppler effect, the Inmarsat team, in conjunction with the accident investigation team, spent ten days refining its work before it briefed Malaysian Prime Minister Najib Razak, who stunned the world by revealing the plane's flight had ended in the south Indian Ocean. This and other information spawned conspiracy theories all across the Internet, some of which include:

The CIA knows the whereabouts of Malaysia 370 (yeah, right), a claim made by the former Malaysian prime minister.

The plane landed at Diego Garcia, a military base located on a small atoll in the Indian Ocean.

It was hijacked to Afghanistan, and the passengers are being held captive.

It was hidden under another airplane while airborne to avoid radar detection.

It was abducted by aliens.

The missing plane was an elaborate insurance scam (a theory put forth by the Malaysian police).

The entire event was masterminded by the "Illuminati" (various organizations/individuals who allegedly conspire to control world affairs. Theorists claim this includes some United States presidents and in recent times, the Vatican).

Chinese authorities captured the plane and kidnapped those aboard to uncover more about Edward Snowden's revelations.

It was hidden as part of an electronic warfare experiment.

A military takeout was at work.

A government (which government depends on the theorist) had a secret weapon that can pluck airplanes out of the sky without a trace.

The pilot committed suicide.

There are cracks in Boeing 777s that can lead to a mid-air breakup or a catastrophic drop in pressure.

Terrorists crashed the plane into the sea.

In the end, it's the old "who really shot President Kennedy?" debate all over again. I don't have the answers, but I think what I'm about to propose makes sense.

After watching the extensive media coverage from the point of view of an experienced airline captain who understands most of what's being discussed, I've concluded that no explanation I've heard makes sense. Each theory falls short somewhere with some fact that doesn't fit and ultimately raises more questions than it answers. There's a hole in every single explanation put forth by the TV pundits and airline or government officials. Because none of the pieces completes the puzzle, we need to think differently. One view takes into account twelve unique locations on the planet and unexplained events associated with them.

- Southern Japan – the Dragon's Triangle. Disappearance of the Kaio Maru, a research ship with a crew of thirty-one in 1952.
- Wharton Basin – deep in the Indian Ocean. Disappearance of Malaysia 370
- Loyalty Islands – New Caledonia in the South Pacific northeast of Australia. Sandy Island, a part of New Caledonia, couldn't be found where it had been marked on charts for more than two hundred years. In 2012, the Australian research ship R/V Southern Surveyor traversed the area and found no island, according to multiple news reports. Did it disappear, or was this a very old charting error?
- Hawaiian Islands – Disappearance of a Pan Am airliner in the 1950s.
- Easter Island – a Polynesian island in the South Pacific off the west coast of South America. Disappearance of the population attributed to massive deforestation and other causes.
- Bermuda Triangle, also known as the "Devil's Triangle" – off the coast of Florida. Unexplained disappearance of many planes and ships.
- East of Rio de Janeiro – Crash of Air France 447, an Airbus 330 en route to Paris after takeoff in 2009.
- Sahara Desert south of Algeria – Crash of an Air Algerie McDonnell Douglas MD-80 in 2014.
- Southeast Africa, the North Pole, and the South Pole.

These twelve locations are known as the "Vile Vortices" or the "Devil's Graveyards" because of the unexplained disappearances of ships, planes, and people connected to them. According to a Wikipedia entry, the research of Ivan Sanderson, a Scottish biologist and zoologist who also holds a degree in botany, indicates there are twelve vortices, which can

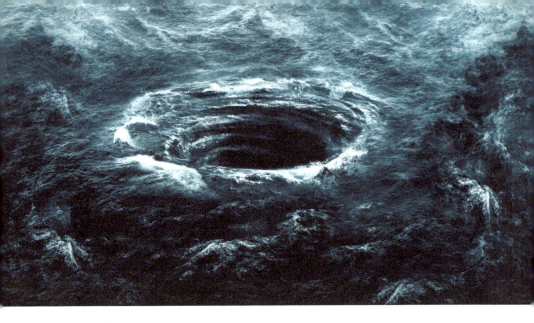

Vile Vortice whirlpool

be air, water, or gas, that take on a spiral effect similar to a whirlpool or a hurricane, and are known as "Vile Vortices." The most common one is the Bermuda Triangle. They are spread evenly around the globe in a deliberate pattern, according to this hypothesis. Besides the ones at the North and South Poles, five are situated above the equator along the same latitude, and five are below the equator along the same line of latitude. This pattern can be connected by straight lines referred to as "ley lines," and are often associated with the presence of something spiritual such as sacred or ritualistic sites, or in this case, energy. Seemingly, the electromagnetic field that occurs around the earth is stronger at these twelve points than anywhere else. Although there is still much we don't know about the laws of physics, our knowledge is increasing exponentially. Here's what we do know about the Earth's magnetic fields:

The inner core of the Earth, which is about two-thirds the size of the Moon, is made mostly of iron. Although it's hotter than ten thousand degrees Fahrenheit, it doesn't liquefy because of the enormous pressure of gravity. Surrounding that core is a twelve-hundred-mile-thick layer of nickel and more iron, but this layer is liquid. The difference in temperature and pressure between the solid inner core and the liquid outer core produces currents in the outer core known as the Coriolis Effect. As the liquid iron flows, it creates electric currents that produce magnetic fields. Subsequently, charged metals that penetrate these fields create their own sub-fields in an endless cycle. All of these fields align pretty much in the same direction and combine to create one vast magnetic field that engulfs the entire Earth.

So I'll add another hypothesis to the dozens circulating about Malaysia 370, although not one to which I particularly subscribe: It could have been affected by the strong magnetic field at the Wharton Basin Vortex in the Indian Ocean. Whatever the initial problem onboard, it may have been tied to these electromagnetic anomalies, which can cause the failure of certain equipment. The initial problem would then have compounded into multiple problems, as is usually the case. Airliners are made of a million parts that must work together perfectly, and if one goes awry, it can trigger a chain of events that is sometimes unstoppable. It often amazes me that statistically we don't have more airborne catastrophes. Conversely, I also believe that flying is safer than freeway rush-hour traffic. Although I've mentioned the advantages of driving over flying, a significant advantage of flying is that it's more regulated than vehicular traffic, including our air traffic control system. Airline maintenance is also scrutinized and controlled, unlike with cars, some of which haven't seen the inside of a mechanic shop in years. Furthermore, there are rarely the loose cannons at the controls of an airplane that you commonly find behind the wheel of a car. Summary: I feel safer in a plane than I do in a car. Then again, cars don't have to worry about vortices.

As intrigued as I am by the idea that the Vile Vortices may have claimed another one, I intuitively feel that in this case it wasn't the vortices, but something else—an emergency, probably a fire, that caused the pilots to turn back toward Kuala Lumpur. If it was a fire, it was probably in the electronics bay in the belly of the airplane, below the cockpit. This would explain why other pieces of equipment failed, such as the transponder.

Once it was hit with whatever problem it was hit with, MH370 kept flying until it ran out of fuel and then crashed in a remote and very deep part of the Indian Ocean. I believe that by that time every soul onboard had been dead for hours because of what was stored in the cargo hold—five thousand pounds of lithium-ion batteries. My guess is those batteries leaked, probably from a fire, and lethal fumes crept into the cabin, where the air is recycled every three minutes. This created a mist-cloud inside the cabin that killed everyone, including the pilots.

Because the plane crashed in a remote and deep part of the ocean, it may take years to locate the black box (which is orange), if ever. My guess is that somewhere down the road, a piece of floating wreckage will wash up on some shoreline, some random person will find it, and it will be identified as a piece of that 777 known as MH370. Once the black box is found, we will know whose theories were right and whose were wrong. I guarantee it will be a completely logical explanation.

CRASH #5: AIR ASIA FLIGHT 8501; OVER THE JAVA SEA

Less than a year after the Malaysian plane went down, AirAsia Flight 8501, heading from Surabaya, Indonesia, to Singapore, disappeared from radar and plunged into the murky waters of the Java Sea with

162 people onboard. Both crashes occurred in an area known as the Intertropical Convergence Zone (ITCZ), which lies near the equator and is prone to monsoonal weather patterns, including violent thunderstorms with vertical updrafts strong enough to overpower a plane. These storms and updrafts build as fast as hell, and in the worst scenarios render a pilot helpless.

These airline accidents are only a few of many that have occurred during my career as a pilot. I had a couple of close calls, and I always found myself praying that I could make it to the end of my career without being one of those poor souls who goes down. I didn't live in fear, I simply accepted it as a risk inherent in a profession like flying. Still, it was inevitable that with each new crash I, like every other pilot, envisioned myself in the same scenario. I've imagined many times what it must feel like to be careening toward the ground at hundreds of miles per hour upside down without one ounce of control, responsible for hundreds of lives, and knowing that it will soon be "fade to black." Once that airplane reaches zero recovery point, I would have had no choice but to accept it, and with it the indescribable horror and adrenaline rush that must accompany the last few minutes of life. I would think I'd also be aware that I'd lost the opportunity to say goodbye to the people I care about. However, after the initial panic, I suspect I would arrive at a place of utter peace. This is apparently not uncommon. Some crash survivors, although not all, say that a state of calm and serenity descends on them right before the moment of perceived death. Since I believe this would be physical death and that the soul lives on and remains conscious, I can hope to have the same experience; it's perhaps that heightened awareness that accounts for peace and acceptance.

Another consolation is that many, if not most, crashes result in instant death. If the plane hits water, as was the case with Malaysian Flight

370 and AirAsia Flight 8501, the impact is as forceful as one with solid ground, due to surface tension of water. The key difference between a crash on water and one on land is that in water most of the debris will sink, excluding that which is designed to float, such as seat cushions, and in the unlikely event that anyone survives the crash, they would probably drown. However, so unimaginable are the G-forces, no one on board would feel the impact or the almost instant annihilation that follows.

After crashes like these on land, the impact crater, also known as a "smoking hole" in aviation parlance, is surprisingly small and belies the magnitude of the horror and loss. More apt is the shape of the crater. Thanks to the fuselage and wings, it resembles a cross.

CHAPTER TEN
BRAVING THE ELEMENTS #1: HOW THE WIND BLOWS

One of the things I love most about flying is that I always need to be ready for the unexpected. That means I always have to be thinking about multiple things at once, which I find mentally challenging and stimulating. There's no better example than when I'm landing on a runway in a stiff crosswind. Runways are engineered to face in the direction of the commonly prevailing winds at the airport, or in other words, into the headwind. For instance, the winds at SFO (San Francisco International Airport) come out of the west for most of the year. The magnetic heading for west is 270 degrees. Therefore, two runways, 28 right and left, are constructed so that pilots land toward the west and as directly into the wind as possible. There is enough air traffic density, especially during peak periods, to justify the building of two runways. Since the winds at SFO come from a 280-degree direction most of the time, both accommodate a landing in that direction. However, there are times when the wind may be coming from a slightly different direction, which explains the existence of the runways labeled 01 right and left. There is also a set of runways for winds from the south called 19 left and right, which are the same concrete strips as the 01 runways, but planes land on them in the opposite direction. It can get complicated.

A pilot never wants to land with a tailwind unless a dire emergency, such as an onboard fire, demands that he get the plane on the ground as quickly as possible. Added wind on the tail of the plane will push it much farther down the runway than would be the case in a headwind and requires extra runway length. United has a ten-knot-tailwind limitation; beyond that, landing distance becomes a concern.

Landing into a crosswind presents other challenges. For example, if I'm landing on Runway 28 right, which is labeled in bold white paint appearing as 28R, I would optimally want a 280-degree wind. We don't live in a perfect world, however, especially when nature is dictating the terms. We could be landing with a wind coming from a direction of 320 degrees (a northwest wind), which would give us a forty-degree-right crosswind. Wind from that direction is still primarily a headwind, but a quartering headwind. The most pronounced crosswind would be 90 degrees. If it were a right 90-degree crosswind, it ceases to be a headwind. United has a 36-knot-crosswind limitation. If the wind shifts to a tailwind, the control tower initiates a runway change to the 19s, where the wind would be a headwind. Because airplane arrivals and departures are important to airport traffic flow, the normal mode of operation at SFO is to conduct simultaneous takeoffs and landings for narrow-bodies on runways 01R/01L and for wide-bodies on runways 28R/28L with appropriate spacing so no one runs into anyone. Narita Airport in Tokyo, however, is a different animal altogether. The winds are almost always crosswinds, and they're always variable and squirrelly, routinely reaching peak gusts of twenty-five to forty miles per hour.

Preparation for a stiff crosswind landing usually starts early, maybe 150 miles from the airport and before the aircraft has initiated a descent from cruise altitude. The mechanics of a crosswind landing include two possible maneuvers—a "side slip" or a "forward slip."

In a side slip, the airplane is slightly banked into the crosswind with the upwind wing lowered and use of the opposite rudder to cancel out any drift, thus keeping the plane straight and level. The objective is to keep the plane dead center over the painted white centerline of the runway. Without that opposite rudder, the airplane would drift outside the confines of the runway before touch down, obviously making a landing impossible. In this maneuver, the upwind main landing gear touches the concrete before the left main landing gear does.

In the forward-slip maneuver, the airplane isn't banked, and the nose is not pointing down the center line of the runway as in the side slip; it's a nose "off-center" landing. The pilot lands with both wings level, but this time instead of using a lowered left wing and the opposite rudder to counter the drift, the pilot turns the nose of the airplane upwind, or into the wind, and counters the drift with the downwind rudder. We correct the off-center heading and realign the nose with the centerline of the runway at the last second before touch down. In the case of the 747, there are four separate sets of "landing gear trucks," and the inboard set can swivel, therefore allowing the plane to land in that off-center heading and self-correct after touch down. Many pilots choose not to land the 747 that way, also known as a "crabbed" position, but instead, at the last second before touch down, swing the nose of the airplane back over the centerline using the downwind rudder and land on all four gear trucks simultaneously.

One of the fun aspects of this last-second correction out of a forward slip or "crab angle," is that when the plane is in a "crab," the flight crew's bodies are not over the runway, but over the grass off to the upwind side of the runway. That's because the landing gear in the 747 is so far back along the fuselage and behind the cockpit that when the main wheels are over the runway centerline, the cockpit is over the grass. When the nose swings back to centerline, it's a similar effect to taking a video and panning the camera quickly to the left or right, so that the surrounding imagery in the frame passes you by in a blur. Finally, when you stop panning, there you are. The centerline is right in front of you. This is why, when trained in the simulator for this maneuver, instructors suggest that the crew align their butts with the lights on the upwind runway, and not the centerline. It's disconcerting, but with a lot of practice, it becomes muscle memory.

Many times, conditions will dictate variations and degrees of both the side slip and forward slip in combination. Because the plane is moving fast during a landing phase, usually between 145 and 160 knots depending on the flap setting and weight, pilots don't have the luxury of overthinking these maneuvers. There's simply no time for processing. It has to be performed with experience, intuition, and your own kinesthetic sense of the plane.

The feeling I love most about "slipping" is the sense that I'm being pulled and pushed simultaneously because these maneuvers exert varying degrees of centrifugal and centripetal forces. When pilots maneuver the upwind wing, they're exerting an opposite force with the downwind rudder. It feels a little like the teacup ride at Disneyland.

CHAPTER ELEVEN
PRETTY IS AS PRETTY FLIES

Right next door to Cort Aviation, where I worked and ultimately became part owner, was another flight school and charter operation that had something we didn't have—a beautiful, twin-engine Cessna 310.

Cessna 310

I had never flown a multi-engine airplane before and was itching to get behind the controls of that thing and fly it. Finally, I walked over one day and introduced myself to the owners, who recognized me immediately. For months they'd seen me on the ramp getting in and out of Cessna 150s, either conducting flight instruction or giving demo flights to prospective clients. After a little conversation, I was thrilled when they asked me if I would be interested in flying the Cessna 310 on routine trips to the Bahamas. I jumped at the opportunity, and soon we were talking about the specifics. I would be making one run a week to Nassau and earning more than I could as an instructor. And by the way, they added, I would be carrying a cargo of marijuana.

I politely declined the offer, citing the risk to my dreams of becoming an airline pilot. They responded that they understood completely, however, if I ever discussed their offer with anybody else, they would break my legs.

At a later date, I did have the opportunity to fly that Cessna 310. One summer, my charter neighbors found themselves with a lot of charter business and a shortage of pilots, so the owners offered me a legitimate charter flight to Nassau. I quickly agreed. After only about forty hours in the air, I began to realize that this beautiful twin-engine airplane lacked the power of many other twin-engine airplanes. I began to tire of flying it.

Isn't life a little like that? How many people have fallen for someone based solely on physical attraction only to find that boredom set in after the honeymoon phase? Then they find themselves trying to remember what it was that caused them to fall in love in the first place. If that person doesn't *elevate* your life, if the relationship is underpowered and not climbing well like that Cessna 310, then something probably needs to change. The same principle holds for material possessions that people accumulate as status symbols. Pretty at first, then meaningless. I can remember many times I bought "man toys" and quickly grew tired of them, a memory that makes it impossible for me to look at someone with a collection of fancy possessions or a so-called trophy wife/girlfriend and feel any envy.

In the case of the 310, I continued to fly it anyway. I needed the multi-engine flight time in my logbook to improve my resume, always with an eye toward that elusive goal of one day being an airline pilot.

CHAPTER TWELVE
HIGH JINKS ON HIGH

One of the keys to life, and one of the hardest to achieve, is to take it lightly and find the humor in your experiences, even in the mistakes, losses, and apparent setbacks. Pilots seem especially good at this; perhaps they need it to withstand the pressures of the job. It makes sense that people in any given profession would share common personality traits, especially in specialized professions. And as far as pilots go, I'd say that most are pretty smart guys, many a bit rebellious, and almost all have a great sense of humor. Even those serious- and conservative-looking pilots you see walking in the terminal have a tremendous sense of humor, in a reserved sort of way. I'd say I have something of a sarcastic sense of humor. I make light of almost everything, love to make people laugh, and love to laugh at myself. I also have a penchant for practical jokes. I've often visited joke shops to buy props like those gadgets that you can tape to a ten-dollar bill and can reel in when somebody bends over to pick up the bill. I've flown with other pilots who bring things from joke shops and then spring some pretty wild gags on unsuspecting flight attendants. Being the jokester I am, it puts me on the floor in tears when they unwittingly bend down to pick up the tethered bill. But what goes around comes around.

One day I was walking in my hometown of Coronado when I saw a five-dollar bill blowing around the sidewalk in the wind. I bent over to pick it up, and it was snatched away so quickly that I knew immediately what had happened. Five kids sitting on a nearby bus bench had tricked me with my very own trick. Once I was able to control my laughter, I told them how I used the same ploy on flight attendants, and they laughed, too. I love it when kids are smart alecks—in a good-natured way, that is.

Pilots play all kinds of other harmless games in the cockpit, and not just with flight attendants, but with each other. I was once flying a Boeing 757 from Los Angeles to Boston, and after five hours in the air, we were all a little slaphappy and tired. Boston is a very dense air traffic area with nonstop talk from controllers and pilots. While the copilot was flying, the controller gave us a very long, complicated clearance, which I dutifully wrote down, but when it was my turn to respond, I switched the radio transmitter from VHF 1, which is used to communicate with the controllers, to the cockpit interphone, which only the other pilot can hear. Then, as if talking to the controller, I said, "Don't tell me what the hell to do!" or at least that's a sanitized version of what I said. It shocked the first officer so much he jolted in his seat. Then I switched the radio back to VHF 1, answered the controller with the standard "Roger, United 951" and proceeded to laugh so hard I couldn't speak any further; the now-recovered copilot had to talk for me. Just a silly little joke but a harmless one, and that's how we broke the tedium.

Once in a while, we would hear a pilot on another plane reciting that spiel we normally give to passengers when we're turning off the seatbelt sign, such as the altitude at which we'll be cruising, arrival time, and weather at the destination. He'll go through this litany on the air traffic control channel rather than the PA system. In other words, he's forgotten to switch radios before starting his speech. But do we tell him? Never. It's understood in the airline business that no one, and I mean no one, interrupts this guy, no matter how long he prattles on. It's too entertaining. Usually, the pilot will realize his mistake within fifteen or twenty seconds, but that's enough time to unleash wisecracks from every pilot within a hundred-mile radius. The exchanges can be so hysterical that even the controllers don't interrupt. The victim who has been on the wrong channel will suddenly hear voices from all around him asking:

"What time was that landing again"?

"Can you repeat that, I didn't quite catch it the first time?"

I've even heard controllers say things like, "Sit back, relax, and enjoy the flight," a play on the worst pilot cliché in the industry.

Every pilot who eavesdrops on one of these accidental spiels turns to his flying partner and sarcastically pronounces "I've never done that!" because every pilot has done it at least once, and we all know that. We may laugh at others, but we're just as ready to laugh at ourselves.

The most joking occurred during the four years I worked for People Express Airlines in the 1980s, where everyone was young, and crews stayed together an entire month, thus developing a comfort level with each other that led to a lot of horsing around in the cockpit. That's not to say that we weren't also highly skilled. We had to be—we were operating in and around the New York metropolitan area, which has the highest air traffic density of any place I've flown. This was also in the pre-9/11 days, before things became as intense and scrutinized in the cockpit as they are now. One month, I was flying with a colleague who had a sense of humor very similar to mine, in a plane that was having problems with the magnet that helps hold the cockpit door closed. As usual in a low-cost airline such as People Express, things don't always get fixed as quickly as you would like. Consequently, whenever we'd take off and the nose of the airplane was angled upward due to our climb, the door would fly open. Since very few passengers ever get the chance to see what the pilots are doing during this critical phase of flight, everybody in the aisle seats would eagerly thrust their heads into the aisle and forward to see what the cockpit looked like while we were flying. We loved that—we were in our twenties with young male egos, and we relished the attention. Although I'm almost embarrassed to admit it now, we used to purposely make steep climbs to make that door fly open. Each time, as we climbed out and began to level off, the flight attendant sitting in the forward jump seat had to reach around and slam the flying door shut. We would laugh like crazy over that, and the passengers enjoyed it as much as we did. They told us so when they were getting off the airplane.

We played a few tricks on passengers as well, but only when they deserved it, or at least that's how I rationalized it. On one flight, a flight attendant told me about a contentious passenger who had been giving her a hard time. That's when I came up with the "overhead bin" idea. In a 737, the overhead bin on the left side of the airplane at row one jutted out in a way that when you deplaned through the front door, you had to swing your head to the right to avoid hitting the corner of it. After we landed and pulled into the gate, when the difficult passenger passed by, I said to him, "I hope you had a great flight." I knew that he'd turn his head to the right to see and answer me, and I also knew this would take his attention off the bin. Sure enough, he walked into it head first. Even though I'd set him up, I said, "Uh-oh, watch your head!" all the while howling with laughter inside. I know, I know, it wasn't especially mature, but I got my instant karma many times over with the head knocking that went on in the cockpit. A 737 doesn't exactly have the largest cockpit in aviation, and when we'd climb in and out of our seats, we were always painfully reminded of the overhead panel, which angles forty-five degrees upward right above our head. No matter how aware we were, somehow we always seemed to hit our heads on that thing. Each time, we'd have to look up and make sure we hadn't accidentally flipped a switch on or off with our battered heads. It wasn't especially funny at the time, but that's how it is with humor in life. Sometimes it doesn't seem funny until thirty years later.

Pilots, flight attendants, and controllers have all had their little jokes over the years, but one of the biggest pranksters of all is the invisible, mysterious one that lurks on the cockpit floor. I don't know who or what he is, but he's infamous among pilots. An airline cockpit is like a black hole. It seems to defy logic, but once you drop something, it's likely you'll never see it again. No one seems able to explain this phenomenon, but I have a working hypothesis. The space where we rest our feet in front of the rudder pedals is slick, shiny aluminum that isn't carpeted. Maybe when we drop an object, it bounces onto that surface, slides its way forward and disappears down into the structure of the airplane behind the rudder pedals. Or maybe it bounces somewhere under the seat where anything would be difficult to find because there's not enough floor space to get down there and rummage around. And maybe there is no logical reason at all—maybe it's just that the universe likes to have its little jokes, too.

CHAPTER THIRTEEN
MY NOT-SO-BRILLIANT CAREER AS A BOOTLEGGER

Occasionally I would visit a lobby bar at one of the nicer hotels in Tehran. Some of the other pilots who also were flying with Iran Air under an expatriate contract had recommended the place. In 1977, alcohol was permitted in Tehran, but it was very expensive. Thus, the bartender at this hotel would ask pilots to bring back quart bottles of Johnny Walker Black Scotch from Europe, usually purchased at the duty-free shop. He paid us four times what we paid for it, which was lucrative for us but even more lucrative for him. He made much more money selling the scotch than he'd paid for it. Of course, it wasn't legal for pilots to bring in more scotch than the one or two bottles permitted for "personal use" but we found a way to elude detection. We'd dismantle some of the panels in the cockpit and stow the bottles in the aircraft structure. All we had to do was re-install the panels with a Phillips screwdriver and we were good to go. On one particular flight, I had eight or ten bottles of Johnny Walker hidden behind various panels in the cockpit, but this was nothing compared to the "smuggling" of the Iranian captains, who seemed to know no restraint.

The captain on this flight was known to be, shall we say, fairly rough on the controls, and he made a very hard landing (known as "pranging one on"). I muttered "Jesus" under my breath, and then noticed that the smell of scotch permeating the air in the cockpit, presumably from bottles that hadn't survived the landing. This made me nervous as we made our way from the runway at Mehrabad Airport in Tehran, where I knew what was waiting. Whenever we arrived in Tehran from Europe, Iranian customs officials would board the aircraft and search the airplane thoroughly for contraband. If you're caught doing something illegal in a country like Iran, you get far more than just a slap on the wrist; you could get years in prisons too barbaric to describe, or even execution. So this aroma of alcohol was a real problem. We had a very short span of time after that cruncher of a landing until we reached the gate where customs personnel would board, so we came up with a diversion. We told traffic control that we had a minor problem with the aircraft so the controller would direct us to a remote area of the airport known to pilots and controllers as "the penalty box." Airplanes needing attention are stationed there so they don't block the flow of other airplanes taxiing to the runway for takeoff or to the gate after landing. The "box" can also be used in winter for planes waiting for remote de-icing before takeoff, or it can be used for sorting out a maintenance issue over the radio. One thing is sure: If you go to the penalty box, nothing is going to happen quickly.

While waiting, I was busy in the cockpit with our screwdriver taking the panels off the bulkheads. I mopped up the scotch, collected the broken glass, and crammed the unbroken twenty-five bottles into a duffel bag. I took those bottles to the lavatory and poured them down the toilet. I stashed the empty bottles in the lav and galley trash bins and our suit-cases. Back in the cockpit, I broke a bottle of perfume that one of the flight attendants had purchased in the duty-free shop in Europe (after paying her for it, of course) in hopes the eau de cologne would over-power the eau de scotch. It worked. When customs came aboard, they noticed nothing amiss and didn't even bother to search our suitcases. However, it could have gone the other way, and I could have ended up in an Iranian prison. That was a dumb thing for a 26-year-old to do. I had learned the danger of profiting off illicit activities, and that danger, among others, was a false sense of invincibility. I had believed in my own infallibility and had underestimated the ability of fate to intercede when we're on the wrong course. I had to think fast and act as if I'd had to respond to a TCAS alert (Terminal Collision Avoidance System). Both are high-pressure situations with much at stake, if not handled correctly.

TCAS is standard equipment in airliners and has three functions. It can:

1. Aurally issue a TA (traffic advisory), for which no evasive maneuver is required. TCAS alerts pilots to threatening traffic within twenty to forty-eight seconds of the clos-est point of approach. The alert says "Traffic, traffic" in a moderate volume over our speakers in the cockpit.
2. Aurally issue an RA (resolution advisory), which requires pilots to respond within five seconds and to deviate from the last air traffic control clearance. In this case, the voice yells, "CLIMB, CLIMB" or "DESCEND, DESCEND."
3. Aurally issue a "clear of conflict advisory," once the plane has achieved adequate vertical separation from the intrud-ing aircraft, following an RA. At that point, pilots can re-turn to ATC clearance.

TCAS is tied into the FD (flight director), which presents a digital display of red crosshairs on the PFD (pilot flight display), similar to what you would see looking through a rifle scope. The FD bars move to provide pitch and bank guidance—how many degrees to pitch the nose up or down, or how many degrees of bank to execute an evasive maneuver. The crew disconnects the autopilot to perform this maneuver because it's a lot faster to fly it by hand. Of course, once pilots are hand flying, the possibility exists that in the heat of battle they can over-correct or over-control the airplane, pulling too many G's (short for gravity). This is the sensation one feels on a wild roller coaster, but in an airplane, it can injure passengers, and damage the aircraft and control surfaces critical for flight. This is precisely why airliners have FDs.

Rest assured that good reactions and responses are a matter of muscle memory, which is a function of training and practice. This stuff isn't magic. And it taught me how to stay cool in high-pressure situations in daily life as well. It's a trait worth developing, and life offers no shortage of practice opportunities. If you do exercise your own internal TCAS, before you know it, you'll be able to avoid some of life's collisions, operating just on auto.

CHAPTER FOURTEEN
THE YEAR OF THE HOT CHICKS

From 1974 to 1975, I was pretty much flying with as many students as I could to build up flight time. In the aviation profession, the sequence of licensing is private pilot, instrument rating, multi-engine rating, flight instructor, flight instructor for instruments, and Airline Transport Pilot Certificate, or ATP. To get an ATP, you need 1,500 hours of flight time. That's the first big hurdle, and I was overcoming it with my teaching hours, but not overcoming it happily. To break up the monotony of flying six to eight hours a day with students, I had to add some interest to my life, and I did it by taking odd jobs once a week with other flight operations around the Hollywood-Fort Lauderdale area. That's what led me to "Corrosion Corner."

Corrosion Corner is an area in the northeast corner of Miami International Airport where old airplanes sit around waiting for a buyer to either renovate them or turn them into scrap metal. There were some shoddy-looking hangars where minimal maintenance work was performed, and some makeshift offices for the companies that owned the planes. All kinds of struggling, starving pilots would routinely cruise the Corner looking for any kind of flying job, and especially looking for experience with larger airplanes, which was considered more valuable to a potential airline employer. When I dropped by Corrosion Corner, there was a big, beautiful DC-3 sitting there that was in surprisingly good condition. That's what motivated me to walk into one of the offices, introduce myself, and give the manager my resume. He said he was looking for a guy to fly as copilot once or twice a week to Nassau with crates full of chicks for the poultry industry there, and I immediately signed on. Never had I imagined how loud two hundred crates full of chirping chicks could sound inside the fuselage of a DC-3, even over the noise of the two gigantic engines and their propellers. Neither had I imagined the smell. Once we arrived in the triple-digit heat of Nassau, it was necessary to offload the chicks rapidly, or they would die of heat prostration. Unfortunately, the definition of speed in Bahamian culture wasn't quite the same as in, say, New York City. Watching the ground crew in frustration, it seemed to me they made snails look supersonic. Many of the little chicks died, making the already rank smell even worse.

I was sorry for the chicks, but the flights to Nassau were a remedy for the tedious days when I was earning my stripes by teaching, all the while yearning to be an airline pilot. By finding an interest on the side, I was able to remain optimistic, engaged, and focused on my goal.

But I can still remember the smell . . .

Baby chicks in a crate

CHAPTER FIFTEEN

THE FLIGHT THAT SHOULDN'T HAVE BEEN

One day at my flight school, Cort Aviation, I was flying a charter in a Piper Apache that I would call a beater. The plane smelled mildewed, like the inside of an old car, and it didn't have very much in the way of good navigational equipment. But I needed flight time, so I wasn't about to argue about flying an old crate. Also, I figured that if anything unexpected happened, I would never be far from civilization and could probably be rescued. That's where I miscalculated. I was sent over the Atlantic to an obscure town called Rock Sound on one of the Bahamian islands, about 260 miles from Hollywood-Fort Lauderdale. Rock Sound, with its breathtaking views, dramatic cliffs, pink sandy beaches, shady trees, and snorkeling, is an ideal retreat, but not the best destination when you're flying a beater. In that part of the world, there aren't many navaids, the ground-based equipment with which you navigate your aircraft. I had only an ADF (automatic direction finder), a primitive instrument by today's standards, and not all that accurate, especially over the ocean. However, I was young, ambitious, and probably a little reckless, so I took the plane anyway, with four paying passengers in the back seat. The problems started about two hours into the flight when according to the ADF, I should have been over Rock Sound. Instead, I was over a vast empty expanse of ocean, with no land in sight, and not enough fuel to look for it and also make the return flight. I began to get nervous and could feel myself sweating—what is known in the aviation business as "sucking up seat cushion." I had to make a decision, and I had to do it quickly—either abandon looking for Rock Sound or continue searching and risk ending up like Amelia Earhart. I turned the plane around and headed back to North Perry Airport, while I still had the fuel to do so.

I had made a mistake. I had settled for something substandard because I had allowed my emotions and ambitions to override my common sense. Now, I never settle for substandard, and that applies to planes, relationships, work, and anything else in life. It's better that we trust our gut or, if it's already too late, turn around and direct ourselves back home. Soon enough, another and better plane will be waiting.

CHAPTER SIXTEEN
PILOTS –
THE ULTIMATE ACHIEVERS

I have flown with many pilots in the course of my career. If the trip was over twelve hours long, there were four of us in the cockpit—three first officers, two of whom served as relief pilots, and me, the captain.

Normally, the first officer and I were alone for six hours while the relief pilots were in the bunk room, sleeping. In six hours, you tend to get into deep conversations and to learn a lot about your flying partner: his marital status, the kind of house he lives in, his hobbies, his finances, and more. There's a vast range of lifestyles among pilots, as I suppose there are in most professions. Some guys live way beyond their means and others below. Some are divorced and travel solo on their days off, and others have been married a long time and travel with their wives. Many even bring their wives on work trips with them. Still others are paying for their kid's college tuition and don't have the discretionary income for pleasure trips. They all have different personalities, temperaments, and philosophies. But if there's one common trait throughout the pilot community it's this: they can master anything they set their minds to. If there was ever a group of overachievers, this is it.

I've flown with many pilots who own businesses on the side, including one who grew grapes in the wine country of California. I was part of that group, owning a furniture company specializing in unique bedroom furniture for teenagers. I've flown with pilots who are also attorneys, accountants, and doctors. Many of them have adventurous pasts, such as those who flew fighters based on aircraft carriers, one of the most difficult and scariest jobs in aviation. What has always amazed me about pilots is the vast skill set they've accumulated in their lives, from the most practical to the most exotic.

For example, if I found myself in a conversation with a pilot about our houses, I might discover that he wired his home for electricity and laid out all the piping for the plumbing himself. At first, whenever I heard those stories, I'd invariably ask, "How the hell did you learn all that stuff? From your dad?" I would ask that because I'd grown up without a father and was curious to know if these skills were part of everything else I'd missed. As it turns out, they weren't. Surprisingly, most pilots say they learned these skills on their own, usually from reading books and magazines. So often have I heard such stories that it began to feel like a common denominator among pilots—they're self-learners. I've even known pilots who built airplanes, completely restored cars, or crafted beautiful furniture. And it's not just the case at United; I found it was just as common when I talked to pilots in the airlines I used for commuting, including Southwest, Virgin America, and US Airways.

Here is where I don't fit the typical pilot profile: I can't do any of that stuff. But I'd always wondered if I could. If I put my mind to it, could I run electrical wiring through a house or lay out all the plumbing? I got my answer, indirectly, during the economic crash late in 2008 when my furniture business was beginning to fail.

At first, I thought the company's decline meant I lacked the proper business skills. Later, I realized the real problem was that my company sold luxury items and such businesses are the first to go bankrupt during a recession. Still, before I came to that realization, I decided to do something proactive about the problem; I would go back to school and get an MBA.

To get accepted into an appropriate university, I had to take some prerequisite tests, so I went to my local bookstore and bought the best preparatory books I could find. There were tests on comprehension, science, and math, but it was the latter that made me wince. In high school, I found math difficult and squeaked by in algebra with just C's or D's.

Being the type of person I am, and having that typical pilot determination, I jumped into my new project with both feet. I reset my thinking on algebra, cleared away the past, and started over. When I started with the basic algebra section, I was surprised to discover how easily it went if I focused and concentrated a bit, neither of which I could manage in high school. Once I had the foundational understanding and progressed into more advanced algebra, it got easier, not harder. For years I'd assumed I was poor at algebra because I lacked the capacity, but now it was clear that only motivation had been missing. The recession had finally offered what high school could not. Algebra convinced me that I could be good at anything I put my mind to, as long as I could give it proper focus and was fueled with desire. I've put my mind to many other things since then, but never all at once. Someone once told me "you can do anything, but you can't do everything." I believe that. Now I'll try anything, but I limit myself to no more than two pursuits at a time.

After mastering algebra, I could see how some of my fellow pilots learned to do electrical and plumbing work. My interests just happen to be different. For me, it's all about music and writing right now, which I find to be a little ironic since piloting is a very left-brain pursuit, whereas music and writing are associated more with the creative, right brain. In reality, however, music is mathematical in theory. It's therefore a highly left-brain pursuit with an element of creative right brain thrown in, especially if composing is involved. Writing is also largely a left-brain function; there are very specific skills involved in structuring words and organizing material in the most compelling way. But like anything, if you truly want to learn it, you can. This was true for me with flying as well. I found it difficult at first, but each skill got easier with practice, and within a couple of years, it became as natural as driving a car.

In any event, through algebra, music, writing, flying, and everything else I've done in life, I've come to believe that anyone can indeed do anything they set their mind to if they're willing to invest the time and energy and to summon up some passion. It's the pilot approach to life. And I highly recommend it.

CHAPTER SEVENTEEN
BRAVING THE ELEMENTS #2: ROCKY TIMES OVER THE ROCKIES

America may be beautiful for its spacious skies and purple mountain majesties, but that beauty can be a challenge for an airline pilot. I was based in Denver from 1986 to 1999, which meant that each time I flew in or out, I was crossing the Rocky Mountains, which offers stunning views, yes, but also some very strange weather patterns. A pilot can get into trouble quickly if he's not aware of some of the pitfalls of mountain flying.

Normally when we take off from Denver International Airport, we're heading west and find ourselves almost immediately over the Rockies.

Almost invariably, the second you reach those mountains the air starts to get bumpy. That's because we're flying through the three-thousand-mile-long Continental Divide, which runs south-north from Mexico to Canada. About 650 of those miles run through Colorado. The

Denver Rocky Mountain front range

Rocky Mountain overflight

Continental Divide is a demarcation line for America's rivers, with those west of the divide flowing into the Pacific Ocean and those on the east side flowing into the Atlantic Ocean. But it's not water that concerns pilots; it's air.

Some weather patterns are of great concern when flying across mountain ranges, and that includes not just the Rockies, but the Tetons and the Cascades.

The first anomaly is a "mountain wave." Mountain waves occur when large-scale winds are blowing perpendicular to the range. It's similar to the way fast-moving water flows over a large boulder in a river. As the river current flows over the stationary boulder, waves are formed downstream of the boulder. Wind does the same thing when it encounters a large mountain range; it's forced to rise over the mountains and immediately descend on the other side in the form of a wave, creating turbulence that can make it difficult to control a plane. It can force an aircraft to deviate from its assigned altitude, which is known as an "altitude bust." If the turbulence is severe enough, it can produce dangerous hail, create icing, over-stress the elevators, or cause injury to the passengers.

Another wave that doesn't make for smooth surfing is the hydraulic jump induced wave, which has also been seen in the Sierra Nevada and ranges in Southern California.

The "jump" wave forms when there is a lower layer of dense air. After air flows over the mountain, a type of shock wave forms at the trough or bottom of the flow, where the air hits the bottom and bounces up at a very high velocity. Then it hits the slower velocity air above it, and that's when the trouble starts. That higher velocity air can "jump" up many times higher than the mountain itself, and it's no place for a plane to be. This hydraulic jump is similar to a rotor, spinning air like a hurricane and causing severe turbulence.

The hydraulic jump can be seen—it's distinguished by towering roll clouds, or lenticular clouds (so named because they look like the lenses of glasses). They're very dangerous and must be avoided at all costs. A jump wave can easily upset an airplane and end in a crash if the pilot isn't properly trained and aware.

Lenticular cloud

Another threat in mountain flying is the occurrence of wind shear, that strong downdraft of air from a towering column of cumulus clouds that extends to the ground. Although very dangerous to airplanes, advanced predictive warning systems now exist.

And finally, there's always the possibility of clear air turbulence, or CAT, which isn't associated with clouds and therefore can't be detected by radar.

One of the most visually stunning experiences in flying over places like Denver has nothing to do with meteorology and is caused by airplanes themselves. Those would be the long, white wispy trails in the sky you sometimes see when a jet passes overhead, technically known as "contrail arrays." They're actually ice clouds, formed when water vapor shoots out of the jet's tailpipe. The vapor condenses into small droplets, which then freeze in the fifty- to sixty-below-zero temperatures of the upper atmosphere.

In areas with a lot of air traffic, like Denver, the sky is a beautiful display of multiple contrails crisscrossing each other like a random maze of tic-tac-toe boards.

Contrails

Strangely enough, these airy brush strokes in the sky have become the source of a conspiracy theory. Some people refer to contrails as "chemtrails" and claim they contain deadly biological agents that are being deliberately sprayed into the atmosphere in a secret plot by the government. I'm an open-minded man, but I'm also a logical man, and so I have to ask: Why would the government want to do this?

One answer offered by conspiracy theorists is that the government is seeding clouds to help avert weather patterns that could be dangerous to the environment. Call me crazy, but wouldn't the hole in the ozone caused by such chemicals be more devastating to the planet than local meteorology? As of 2017, NASA reported, the ozone hole over Antarctica was a little more than 8.9 million square miles, which is slightly smaller than North America.

I can support conspiracy theories about the Kennedy assassination and UFOs, but when it comes to "chemtrails," the explanations don't pass muster. The cost to the health of human beings and the damage to the atmosphere would be so great that one has to wonder why the government would be willing to do this. It would simply be trading one disaster for another, and I feel sure there are enough sane experts in this field who would have made that clear. In the words of Sigmund Freud, "sometimes a cigar is just a cigar" (there are those who say Freud never really did say this, but that's a conspiracy theory for another day).

Contrail patterns

CHAPTER EIGHTEEN

MORE ON AIRASIA FLIGHT 8501 – WHEN HUMAN ERROR BECOMES HUMAN TERROR

At the end of December in 2014, a fishing boat spotted airplane debris and human remains floating in the Java Sea. It was the beginning of an investigation that would uncover a flight doomed by misjudgment and mistakes in the cockpit and would lead to reforms in certain aviation procedures as well as investigations into redesigning the "black boxes" that enable rescuers to recover wreckage at sea.

The debris was from AirAsia Flight 8501, the Airbus 320 mentioned earlier in this book that had taken off from Surabaya, Indonesia, on December 28, 2014, and four hours later had disappeared from radar on its route to Singapore. The plane had plunged into the sea, killing all 155 passengers and seven crew members. With the help of the black boxes, investigators pieced together the events that led to the crash, starting with severe weather patterns and escalating toward disaster as the airline and crew made one bad decision after another.

The captain of Flight 8501 was a 53-year-old who had served as a fighter pilot in the Indonesian Air Force and had logged more than 20,000 hours of flight—in other words, an experienced pilot who nonetheless failed to follow safe procedures. When the flight was at 32,000 feet, he noticed a line of thunderstorms approaching just off the coast of Borneo and at 11:04 p.m., the pilot asked the controller for a deviation of fifteen miles to the left to avoid them. He also asked for a climb from 32,000 feet to 38,000 feet. At 11:11 p.m., Jakarta Radar Control asked the pilot for his intended altitude to avoid the thunderstorms and because of other traffic in the vicinity. At 11:12 p.m. the pilot requested 38,000 feet and Jakarta advised the pilot to standby for clearance to climb to a higher altitude. At 11:15 p.m. the Jakarta controller could only give the pilot clearance to climb to 34,000 feet. The controller received no response. Instead, the plane began to climb much too fast. Normally, a plane would climb at about 1,500 to 2,000 feet per minute, but the flight data recorder (FDR) from Flight 8501 indicated the plane was climbing at over 6,000 feet per minute, an incredibly steep climb for a jet airliner. That rate of climb would bleed off airspeed, like driving a car up a steep hill without giving it gas, especially in the thin air at that altitude, and that's exactly what happened. Seemingly, the pilot did not add sufficient power to overcome the steep climb, the plane stalled and began to descend at 1,000 feet per minute, then at 8,000 feet per minute. That's a screaming descent that had to have terrified everyone on board.

Violent pushovers and pull-ups induce gravitational effects (G's) more than a sustained descent or climb. Think of that moment of weightlessness going over the crest in a roller coaster before the big drop. The effects on the human body can be serious. A red-out occurs when the body experiences a negative g-force sufficient to cause a blood flow from the lower parts of the body to the head. It is the inverse effect of a gray-out, where blood flows away from the head to the lower parts of the body. Human beings can take more positive G's than negative. Fighter pilots have been known to take up to nine positive G's before gray-out or blackout, but maybe two to three negative G's before a serious red-out.

United pilots train in the simulator routinely for emergency descents, which become necessary in the case of onboard fires or other crises. Getting an airplane on the ground ASAP is not that violent unless you jam the nose down drastically, which we never do. If AirAsia were spinning on the way down, those last few moments would've been even worse.

In a story published December 31, 2014, shortly after Flight 8501 was found upside down in waters off Borneo, Stephen Buzdygan, a former British Airways pilot, told the London-based Telegraph newspaper that the plane could have hit severe turbulence and then stalled. Buzdygan said the plane probably went into the water upside down because the sea's depth was eighty feet where the wreckage was found, not deep enough for the plane to have flipped after it struck. The out-of-control descent would have been terrifying and would have produced the sorts of G's that aerobatic pilots experience in air shows.

"I would suggest that there was some sort of upset to the aircraft – severe downdrafts or clear air turbulence," Buzdygan told the Telegraph. "They have had some sort of upset and not been able to control it."

The AirAsia pilot also completed one 360-degree turn to the left before the plane disappeared from radar. At first, the AirAsia plane seemed to have disappeared much like Malaysia Flight 370 less than a year earlier, but two days later the fishermen found its debris and a few weeks after that dive teams found the flight data and cockpit voice recorders.

Most intriguing of the data recovered was evidence that the captain was out of his seat during the crash, conducting a rather strange procedure. He was behind the first officer, who was flying the plane, disabling the flight augmentation computer (FAC) by pulling its circuit breaker. The computer had apparently been malfunctioning. The first officer was forty-six years old and was from Martinique, making him a French national. He was considerably less experienced than the captain, with only around 2,000 flying hours with AirAsia.

The FAC system the captain was disabling is a protective device that prevents pilots from exceeding the design limits of the rudder in high-speed flight. At United, pilots aren't allowed to pull a circuit breaker in an airborne plane without permission from maintenance, via radio. Even then, the procedure is just to recycle it, not pull it or permanently cut power to the system.

The captain's action of pulling the FAC circuit breaker seems to have taken the first officer by surprise, as it caused the autopilot to disengage, leaving the first officer flying the airplane manually. At that point, the captain ordered the first officer to "pull down" to lower the nose, but the first officer heard "pull," which caused him to raise the nose. By the time the captain got back into his seat, the airplane had begun climbing at more than 6,000 feet per minute because the first officer pulled up on the nose as instructed. The captain meant "push," which is exactly what the first officer should have done. The very system that would have prevented the rudder from exceeding the design safety limits had been disabled. That is why the nose angled up to begin with. The first officer exacerbated the situation. The stall was recoverable, but in a heavy jet it would take at least 10,000 feet of altitude loss to recover from the stall without exceeding the G limits of the airplane. This is an example of how quickly things can get out of control due to miscommunication in an airplane, and how crashes are usually the result of a series of mishaps, rather than one single cause.

Routing of AirAsia 8501

The changes that followed the AirAsia crash were swift and significant. The air traffic control agency that allowed the plane to take off was replaced. AirAsia didn't have permission to carry out the flight between Surabaya and Singapore on the day of the crash. In my opinion, if the Indonesian Ministry of Transportation knew the weather was bad, it was negligent to allow them to takeoff. Air traffic controllers are supposed to at a minimum issue a warning or an advisory if the weather can present a danger to flight. Also, I suspect that once this thing grew legs in the media, Indonesian officials probably replaced the air

Wreckage of AirAsia 8501 emerging from the Java sea. Oddly, one wing managed to stay attached to the fuselage

controllers to present the image that they were taking action. In addition, weather radar capability was added to many Indonesian air traffic control centers. And because of this crash, and other plane crashes into the sea including Malaysia Flight 370, officials are looking into creating black boxes (FDRs and CVRs) that would break away from an airplane upon a crash and float on the surface of the water. Looking for black boxes on the ocean floor is costly, dangerous, lengthy, and sometimes impossible.

Finally, as a result of the crash of Flight 8501, the National Transportation Safety Committee of Indonesia, which is charged with investigating transportation safety deficiencies, issued a directive that makes it mandatory for pilots to be briefed by the flight operations department before every departure. That includes a thorough report on real-time meteorological conditions pertaining to that flight.

This is where I, as a United pilot, was astonished. It's completely lost on me why such a briefing wasn't mandatory before. United has done it for decades, with help from computer-generated weather prognostic charts, and a full dispatch center that occupies the twenty-sixth floor of Willis Tower (formerly the Sears Tower) in downtown Chicago. I have to believe it was only the expense that prevented AirAsia, or other airlines, from having these safeguards in place earlier. But then again, we're talking about a different culture with different standards and being judgmental, as usual, isn't going to help anybody.

Each crash is different and takes on a life of its own.

CHAPTER NINETEEN
THINK POSITIVE BUT PLAN A GO-AROUND

Pilots don't climb into the cockpit expecting trouble, but they're always ready for it. It may be counterintuitive, but when we're taking off, we're thinking of aborting, and when we're landing, we're thinking about making a go-around. This is because a pilot has very little time to react in most emergencies. If they are not mentally prepared to abort a take-off and to manage a complete stop before the end of the runway, then they have wasted precious seconds in reaction time, and that can lead to disaster. Take Newark Liberty International Airport, for example. At the very end of Runway 4R lies the New Jersey Turnpike. A plane that overshoots that runway joins the urban gridlock of Toyotas and Hondas, and it wouldn't be pretty.

Conversely, if pilots are making an approach, and something happens that makes a go-around necessary, they have to be ready for the particular challenges of some airports. This especially includes airports surrounded by mountains, such as Palm Springs, California, or Jackson Hole, Wyoming, where the Teton Range looms during a go-around or missed approach. Pilots have to plan carefully for a go-around like that and make sure that the climb performance of the airplane is adequate. High altitudes (Jackson Hole sits more than 6,000 feet above sea level) reduce aircraft performance. A pilot needs to come in very high over that range, and since the valley is only eight to fifteen miles wide, he or she has to completely configure the plane with flaps and gear down as soon as the plane clears the mountains and then make a dive for it. It takes a lot of focus and concentration to pull this off, and it's not as easy as it looks or feels from the passenger seat. To a pilot, a go-around at an airport like this is a thrill ride with all the pluses and minuses that term implies.

Mountainous airports such as these are usually classified as "special" airports by United, and therefore pilots are required to complete specialized training before being cleared to fly in or out of them.

Jackson Hole, Wyoming, precarious takeoff

But even in airports with flat terrain, pilots are still thinking about their next move should some contingency arise out of nowhere. After practicing this preventative thinking in aviation, I've learned to apply the same mental process to situations and circumstances in my personal life. *Expect the best and be prepared for the worst.* I even use it when piloting my other favorite vehicle—my road bike. On one recent ride, my front wheel became stuck in the narrow grooves of a sewer grate, bringing the bike to an abrupt halt. I was flipped over the handlebars and broke two ribs. Luckily, I had quickly aimed my fall at the dirt on the right side of the road rather than the asphalt on the left, or my injuries could have been much worse. Still, I learned that even riding a bike requires preventative thinking. I'm aware of the injuries that can happen if a rider isn't thinking in terms of falling and what he might hit, or what he should try to avoid hitting, whether it be concrete, pebbles, or in my case, a sewer grate. There's an element of disaster in my thinking that wasn't there before. And how does that align with the Law of Attraction? Am I not inviting disaster by thinking about it? I look at it this way: I'm not thinking about disaster—that would be a little phobic. I'm thinking about being prepared. The universe is probably relieved. "Oh, good, here's one lesson I don't have to teach him, preparedness." So maybe it backs off. Almost everyone has noticed at some point that when they're prepared for something, that's when it doesn't seem to happen. On a cloudy day, if you remember your umbrella, it won't rain, but it always seems that if you forget your umbrella, it will rain cats and dogs. So, take it from a pilot with forty years' experience—plan your go-arounds in life. And chances are you won't need them.

CHAPTER TWENTY
HEARING VOICES

Anyone who has ever sat on an airplane listening to channel nine knows the language spoken between air traffic controllers and pilots is so lexicon-loaded that it sounds almost alien. The truth is, this lexicon can be just as hard for pilots to learn, especially those who have just come out of the military into civilian aviation. Military-trained pilots make up about a third of private-sector pilots working in the U.S., a percentage that has declined significantly over the last few decades, according to a 2018 story in the Washington Post. For one thing, military pilots operate almost exclusively out of military bases. Each has its own regulations, air traffic controllers, and airspace structure, much of which is restricted to military traffic only. This entire system falls under the category of Special Use Airspace, which includes Prohibited Areas, Restricted Areas, Warning Areas, Military Operations Areas, Alert Areas, Controlled Firing Areas, and National Security Areas.

In contrast, the airspace for commercial airlines is vastly more complex, especially regarding traffic density. Flying in high-density traffic ranks among the leading causes of stress for commercial pilots, in addition to passenger safety concerns, operating aircraft overnight, flying in bad weather, and equipment malfunction. There are roughly 30,000 airline departures every day in the United States, and there could be as many as 5,300 planes in the sky at peak times. Worldwide, those numbers are about 93,000 planes out of 9,000 airports, and it's getting denser all the time.

There's a typical sequence in pilots' interactions with controllers. It starts at the jet bridge when pilots call for clearance, followed by a call to ramp control on the ground to request pushback from the gate. Then pilots contact ground control for taxi clearance to the active runway. To get takeoff clearance, pilots talk to the tower. After takeoff, flight crews are handed off from the tower to departure control. Finally, they're handed off to an Air Route Traffic Control Center, (ARTCC) which controls us while we're en route. There are many such centers along the way. Once out of range of voice controllers, pilots on the 747 go electronic, switching to a system called CPDLC (controller-pilot datalink communications). We don't communicate by voice over this system—it's all done automatically via electronic uploading and downloading between a controller and our flight management computers. Pilots monitor their GPS position using two digital units that provide latitude and longitude. They then check navigation charts to see how the two positions compare to each other. Additionally, every time they pass specific points along a route, known as waypoints, they check their position, time, and fuel state.

Pilots don't go back to voice again until they are no longer over the Atlantic or Pacific, and in radar contact with the first center controller along the route, for example, Tokyo Control. That would be the first time in hours that the crew of a transpacific flight has heard a human voice. Once they go to voice again, they talk to center, approach control, tower, ground control, and ramp for taxi into the gate. They are never on their own out there.

Usually, crews are the busiest with controllers in the departure and arrival corridors. The controllers are talking to everyone at Mach Two speed, issuing clearances in a monotone voice to a sea of airplanes, keeping all of them separated by specific altitudes and lateral distances. For efficiency, they may issue one communication that contains five or six clearances, all of which the crew is expected to repeat back, and I mean fast. There's no room to miss a radio call, or to ask the controller to repeat the clearance in the dense traffic around an airport. I've been reprimanded by the controller, as have others, for screwing up a read-back on a complicated clearance. It makes the controller's life hell when that happens. Pilots are expected to get it. Usually, when crews hear a reprimand directed to someone else they snicker because they understand the heat of the battle.

As would be expected, when crews are in the midst of this pandemonium, they are also preoccupied with flying the airplane. Sometimes they're so focused on what they're doing with the plane that the relentless drone of the controller's voice doesn't register, and they may not understand that a specific clearance was intended for them. When that happened, I would turn to my first officer and say, "Was that for us?" Uh oh! Too late. Here it comes, just like mom yelling at us after catching us red-handed in the refrigerator after the kitchen's been closed for the evening.

Here's what a typical arrival clearance might sound like to a passenger listening to it on channel nine, with translations:

United niner fife one (United 951)

You are cleared to descend flight level two one zero (descend to an altitude of 21,000 feet)

Passing two fife zero, (25,000 feet) slow to two three zero knots. (230 knots)

At Woodside, (an electronic navigational aid on the ground) turn heading zero three zero (30 degrees)

Expect vectors for ILS runway two eight right San Francisco. (expect directions to get lined up for a straight-in approach to Runway 28R)

Contact Norcal approach one three fife decimal four (contact the Norcal Approach controller on frequency 135.4)

In addition to having to repeat all that back to center, the crew has to be intimately familiar with what's going on around them in terms of traffic. They have to know who's in front of them and what their speed is, who's behind them and what their speed is, and where everyone else is around them. They can see all of these airplanes on their TCAS (terminal collision avoidance system). It's similar to what the controller sees on a radar scope. Flight crews can see the relative altitude of other planes. It's a very tense environment.

One thing pilots learn operating in these situations is to couple up, or engage, the autopilot. The 747 has three autopilots. Normally, pilots only engage the center autopilot, putting the entire airplane "out of hands." It's like engaging the cruise control in your car, times ten. Many pilots like to disengage the autopilot at 10,000 feet during the descent then hand fly all the way down to the runway to keep their motor skills sharp, but in a busy environment, it's better to unload so you can think.

The way I handled it was to relax and gather my resources. I found, and so have many other pilots, that when you read back clearances such as the one above in the reverse order of what the controller sent, it was easier to be accurate. Also, it's not uncommon for a pilot to read back the clearance without using the exact formal language in which it was received. No one makes an issue of this even if it's not technically exact because proceeding forward is beneficial for both parties.

This is one reason why, when the Malaysian Flight 370 crash was making the news and reporters made a big deal out of the copilot's casual "all right, good night," I laughed. It was so normal to me as to be completely insignificant.

My suggestion is that whenever you find yourself in situations where things get so intense that one more thing would overload you, just mentally reach up and hit that center autopilot button. Break it down into manageable chunks and deal with the whole mess a step at a time until you come out the other side. Again, it's a process that takes repeated practice but is totally doable.

CHAPTER TWENTY-ONE
GOING TOPLESS

Pilots of today's large jets would have a hard time imagining the early days of aviation when planes had no radios. Today, a radio control box with volume knobs and toggle switches sits next to each pilot. Radio sets include various combinations of VHF (very high frequency for air traffic control), HF (high frequency for long-distance communications), and SATCOM (satellite communications for direct communications with the company from anywhere on the earth). Pilots can listen to or speak from any of these radios anytime they want. An interphone system allows flight crewmembers to speak to each other either over cockpit speakers or through headsets, and a phone handset is set up for pilots to communicate with flight attendants in the cabin. Additionally, a PA system lets pilots speak to the passengers in the cabin.

The majority of the time pilots are on VHF. Normally, all the pilots wear some form of a headset. I used a custom silicone earpiece with a boom microphone attached that went in my left ear. Some guys wear a headset that crosses the top of their head like standard headphones, but with a boom microphone attached. I consider those uncomfortable. I have seen others who wear expensive Bose noise cancellation headsets, specifically made for pilots. As beautiful as those are, they're very bulky. Still others use a headset without a boom mike, and simply pick up a handheld microphone. To each his own.

You may have guessed that all this radio communication coming into an earpiece or headset can sometimes get annoying. For example, I may have my headset on and my speaker switch off, while at the same time the first officer has his speaker switch on. Listening to the voices coming from his speaker at the same time I'm listening to voices coming through my earpiece or headset is very disconcerting. It sounds like an echo chamber with added volume.

Another annoying sound in the cockpit comes from the HF radios. Since they're high frequency, they can generate a tremendous amount of static, depending on atmospheric conditions and time of day. This can cause a lot of discomfort when you're listening through your earpiece.

Still more annoyance occurs when you're wearing your earpiece and another pilot tests his oxygen mask, which creates a loud air rush noise and sometimes a squealing feedback noise. If your earpiece is in your ear when he does that test, it can feel like your eardrum is exploding. Finally, when you're using your earpiece, and you're listening to nonstop chatter by multiple controllers to multiple airplanes, it's not only annoying, it's fatiguing. We need to wear them, however, because the noise of air rushing against the windscreen when an airplane is traveling at 200 or 300 miles an hour can blot out what we need to hear. The earpiece helps isolate the important stuff from some of that assaultive noise, and also makes your hearing reception clearer, since the transmission is directly in your ear and not emanating from overhead speakers.

After takeoff, planes are handed off from the tower to departure control, and then to ARTCC (air route traffic control center, known simply as "center"). Once planes get a certain distance away from the center controller's airspace, things get a little less hectic. At that point, most guys take their earpiece or headset off and turn on their speaker switches.

As with everything else in an airline environment, pilots don't do or say anything without informing the other pilot first. Normally, before I took my earpiece out and turned on my volume switch for the overhead speakers, I said to the other pilot, "I'm going topless." Yes, it's a little humorous, but we have a ton of those kinds of sayings that are specific to us in the cockpit, and once again, humor diffuses stress. I do exactly the same thing outside of my job when I'm under stress. Unless the situation is grave, which is very rare, I gravitate to humor.

CHAPTER TWENTY-TWO
DING, DING, DING, AND MORE DINGS

Nothing in aviation is easy, not even something as simple as telling time. First of all, each pilot has his own clock set to universal coordinated time, known as UTC, and obviously not local time. Pilots can also find takeoff and landing times on the hard copy of the flight plan, but those are in Greenwich Mean Time (GMT), also known as Zulu, or time at the zero meridian. This isn't easy to interpret or calculate in your head. We can also read our landing time on ACARS (aircraft communications addressing and reporting system), which we all heard about during the media coverage of the Malaysian Airlines Flight 370 crash in the Indian Ocean, but this is also displayed in Zulu time.

On the Boeing 747-400 aircraft, as many as eighteen flight attendants are working in various places within the aircraft. As you can imagine, with up to 374 passengers asking what time the plane will land, it must drive the flight attendants crazy. Normally, pilots provide that information to the passengers in a PA announcement upon turning off the seatbelt sign, but no one ever seems to listen. Consequently, flight attendants keep calling the cockpit to ask the same question. That's because when one calls, none of the others know about it. Normally, these calls occur in one period of time, just around the time the passengers want to go to sleep.

When flight attendants called, we heard a chime. Usually on the first call, we would tell them to hold on while we went through the mental gymnastics required to calculate the time we would land in local time for that country, which is never close to what the flight plan told us. It was not uncommon to no sooner hang up the handset, then we would hear another "ding." If we in the cockpit were busy, this nonstop series of chimes could become very aggravating. Yet we had to work and live with the cabin crew for three to five days, so it was best to be patient. Nevertheless, I've heard pilots, including myself, exclaim "Jesus Christ!" when the calls were especially irritating. I learned early on to tell the first flight attendant who called to please pass the landing information along to all the flight attendants.

As with everything else in life, it's better to be patient, tolerant, and affable, especially in a closed environment like an airliner where people are thrust together for long periods of time. The cockpit crew depends on flight attendants for many services, including a periodic check to see if everyone upfront is still awake. And they bring the meals, with the hotness or the coldness of the meal an indication of how much they liked or disliked us!

In all the decades I flew, I seemed to have run into two distinct groups or types of flight attendants—those who hate us, and those who love us. There are as many reasons for hating us as there are flight attendants themselves, but overall, I found that more flight attendants liked us, working so hard to please us that they go even beyond bringing extra goodies to the cockpit. Some are married to pilots. Some just like people. Some may just like the pilot personality type. Who knows? One thing I do know is that if the relationship between the pilots and the flight attendants isn't good, it can be a very long trip.

From these professional relationships, I've taken away a philosophy that I've integrated into my day-to-day life. When I see people who are stressed, angry, indifferent, aloof, or otherwise unpleasant, I try to remember how it feels when I am under stress. If I'm successful at doing that, I can usually diffuse a situation that could otherwise escalate rapidly. Part of this involves not taking somebody else's anger personally but instead realizing that it could be as simple as they're having a lousy day.

CHAPTER TWENTY-THREE
WHEN WORDS GET IN THE WAY

In aviation, there are universal principles, universal designs, and universal procedures . . . but there is no universal language. Many problems, and many potential disasters, occur because someone misunderstood what someone else said.

When a plane is sitting at the gate, specific communication procedures are mandated, and one especially concerned me as a captain: communication with the "ground pushback man" who's outside the airplane right below the copilot's window and is connected to the plane's interphone. It's his responsibility to make sure the tug driver pushes the aircraft back properly and that the area behind the airplane is visibly clear. It may sound simple, but there's a lot of room for potential disaster. While pilots are busy in the cockpit, the man outside is listening through his headset, waiting for the crew to tell him the plane is ready for pushback. The crew has to obtain pushback clearance from ground control first, which can't be done until the plane is ready. Consequently, when he asks about readiness, 99 percent of the time he is told to stand by. Normally at this point, the parking brake is set, and that's where the danger comes into it. If the tug driver begins to push the airplane back with the parking brake set, the tow bar can snap with such force that it could damage an airplane and cause injuries. This happened on one of my planes, and I narrowly escaped being impaled on the tow bar.

This procedure became even riskier when United merged with Continental Airlines in 2010 and airline flight manuals were integrated. Procedures were changed many times while flight operations tried to respond to feedback and smooth out the meshed airline cultures. The result was confusion. Pilots and the man outside in the headphones had earlier procedures solidly committed to memory, so some had a hard time making the changes. For example, after we got pushback clearance, we were supposed to say "Ready for pushback," and the guy on the ground was supposed to answer, "Ready for pushback, release brakes." But more often than not, when I said "Ready for pushback," I heard nothing but stone-cold silence. That's the moment when I thought he was going to push us back without telling us to release the brakes, and I was going to have another close encounter with a tow bar. To avoid that, I would commit the sin of all sins and break with procedure. Instead of waiting for him to ask me, I asked him if he wanted me to release the brakes. Of course, he said yes. Pilots keep writing operational irregularity reports about such matters, but the wheels of change move slowly in a big airline.

Procedures are extremely important in an airline, and I don't break them lightly. So much has to be done that if we don't follow procedures, we're bound to make mistakes that can range from expensive to lethal. It was the changes in procedures that I minded. To make matters worse, every twenty-four months, pilots are required to undergo a "line check," in which a standards captain or line-check airman sits in the cockpit and observes procedures. A pilot who has been conducting them incorrectly out of habit would certainly do the same in front of this guy.

Often, I told the man with the headphone that we were ready for push-back before he asked. I automatically told him that the brakes were still set. But if I said that in front of a line-check airman, I'd be reprimanded for incorrect verbiage. Still, because many issues fall into this miscommunication category, pilots are sometimes required to take matters into their own hands. It's the captain who's ultimately responsible for everything that happens with an airplane, whether or not it's his direct fault, and that responsibility is part of what they're being paid for.

Another exchange that's vulnerable to miscommunication is that between pilots and air traffic controllers, where one little word can make a big difference. Let's say a controller wanted us to climb to 21,000 feet. In air traffic controller jargon, that would sound like:

> "United 951, climb and maintain two one thousand feet." (21,000 feet)

> Or in reverse, "United 951, descend two one thousand feet." (21,000 feet)

Even though I've never heard of it happening at United, I've heard of communications like these that almost ended up in a midair collision. Why? Because a foreign pilot who didn't speak "aviation" English didn't hear the controller say:

> "Descend *two* one thousand feet" (21,000 feet)

> He heard: "descend *to* one thousand feet" (1,000 feet)

Conversely, when in foreign countries, the phraseology is different than what U.S. crews are accustomed to and can be confusing. They're trained to handle it, but the cockpit is a busy and distracting place. A further complication is that meters are used to measure altitude in China, rather than feet. A readout in the cockpit shows both feet and meters, but there's a catch. When flights are cleared to a certain altitude in meters, the instrument by which crews set that altitude can only be read in feet; therefore, feet must be converted to meters using a plastic conversion card that isn't all that easy to look at when you're flying. In China, wind speed is given in meters per second, rather than miles per hour, and all of this in a Mandarin accent. No wonder I had a headache whenever I landed in China, just as I suppose Chinese pilots have when landing in America. Language may not be universal, but stress certainly is.

CHAPTER TWENTY-FOUR

IF MY NECK HURTS
AM I A PSYCHOPATH?

During my career journey, I've interviewed with American, Delta, US Airways, Northwest (now Delta), and United. Every airline has a different format, but back then, part of the interview process was the test that I mentioned earlier, the Minneapolis Multiphasic Personality Inventory exam, or MMPI. I don't remember which airlines administered this test to me, but I do remember that I wanted an airline job desperately. I knew ahead of time that I'd be required to take this test. It's a frequently used clinical testing instrument, one of the most researched psychological tests in existence, and is employed as a screening instrument for certain professions. The MMPI, although not a perfect test, claims to assess personality traits and psychopathology, which is especially useful in screening for high-risk jobs, although its suitability for this purpose has been controversial. The MMPI contains 567 test items and takes about 60 to 90 minutes to complete. It was well-known at the time I was interviewing that the test was often the tiebreaker in a hiring decision.

The ten clinical subscales measured in the MMPI are:

1. Hypochondriasis—poor physical health and gastrointestinal difficulties.
2. Depression—clinical depression, which is characterized by poor morale, lack of hope in the future, and general dissatisfaction with one's life.
3. Hysteria—poor physical health, shyness, cynicism, headaches, and neuroticism.
4. Psychopathic deviation—general social maladjustment and the absence of strongly pleasant experiences.
5. Masculinity/femininity—interests in vocations and hobbies, aesthetic preferences, activity-passivity, and personal sensitivity.
6. Paranoia—interpersonal sensitivity, moral self-righteousness, and suspiciousness.
7. Psychasthenia—inability to resist specific actions or thoughts.
8. Schizophrenia—bizarre thoughts, peculiar perceptions, social alienation, poor familial relationships, difficulties in concentration and impulse control, lack of deep interests, disturbing question of self-worth and self-identity, and sexual difficulties.
9. Hypomania—over-activity, grandiosity, irritability, and egocentricity.
10. Social introversion—Discomfort in social interactions and withdrawal from such interactions when possible. Limited social skills or a preference for being alone or with a small group of friends.

Some true or false questions from the test:

1. I like mechanics magazines.
2. I have a good appetite.
3. I wake up fresh & rested most mornings.
4. I think I would like the work of a librarian.
5. I am easily awakened by noise.
6. I like to read newspaper articles on crime.
7. My hands and feet are usually warm enough.
8. My daily life is full of things that keep me interested.
9. I am about as able to work as I ever was.
10. There seems to be a lump in my throat much of the time.
11. I loved my father.
12. I see things or animals or people around me that others do not see.
13. I wish I could be as happy as others seem to be.
14. I hardly ever feel pain in the back of the neck.
15. I am very strongly attracted to members of my own sex.

You get the idea. Also, there is a scale within the test that can determine whether you're lying. Tests can only be graded by a clinical psychologist, so a few weeks before I figured I would have to take it for an airline, I took it upon myself to find a clinical psychologist who specializes in grading the MMPI. He agreed to administer the test, grade it, and advise me on what questions needed to be "improved upon." It cost me a couple of bucks, but this concerned a multimillion-dollar career and, more importantly, a job I was passionate about. I was confident that I was within the range of normalcy, but I wasn't willing to let a somewhat arbitrary test determine the fate of my career. Instead, I was determined to do everything I could to assure these ten scales measured me within what "they" call the normal range. It worked. Every airline that interviewed me hired me, except for Delta, which I don't believe was among those administering the MMPI.

CHAPTER TWENTY-FIVE
MUMMIES, NAZIS, AND OTHER COCKPIT CHARACTERS

When you settle into your seat on a plane and buckle your seatbelt, you're putting your life in the hands of a complete stranger who's going to carry you 30,000 feet into the air and whisk you through the clouds at 600 miles per hour, with nothing between you and the thin air but a metal tube. Who is this guy? To start with, he's a rigorously trained, skilled, and fit professional who takes your trust with uncommon seriousness. Both United and the FAA make sure of that. But that said, pilots have their share of quirkiness, as does every profession.

When pilots are sitting in a cockpit for three or four hours, or for ten, twelve, or even fourteen hours on an international flight, their personalities begin to emerge, and they run the gamut. I've often flown with stoic, left-brain, nontransparent types of people, what I'd describe as the typical personality type for this profession. I've flown too with super-achiever pilots who were also lawyers, medical doctors, and in one case, a pilot who was both a lawyer and a doctor. Then there's the other end of the spectrum, the eccentrics and oddballs. These characters are infamous from San Francisco to Washington D.C., two of United's pilot bases. Take for example the guy we called "the mummy."

For some reason, the mummy had gotten it into his head that airline pilots have a higher risk of developing cancer because of high-altitude radiation. As a result, he'd drape himself head-to-toe with the linen cloths that cover our meals, thinking it would block out radiation. He's wrong, by the way. Research indicates that pilots are at no higher risk of radiation-induced cancer than anyone else.

Then there's the most notorious character of all, the Hat Nazi. This nutty guy had an agenda with roots back to the 1980s and a notorious CEO named Glenn Tilton. I've survived about a dozen CEOs at United, and the one most other pilots and I will never forget is Tilton, a personification of the age-old battle between the "big guy" and the "little guy," of corporate greed versus the welfare of the worker, and the man who changed forever the relationship between United pilots and their hats.

Tilton came into United with an agenda—to force the company into bankruptcy and strip the pilots of all they had gained. When he arrived on the scene in 2002, pilots hadn't taken raises or contributions to their 401(k) funds for six years in exchange for 55 percent of the outstanding shares of United Airlines. It was the largest employee stock ownership program in American corporate history, and what should have been a triumph for the workers became ruination for many. The carefully engineered bankruptcy wiped out the value of that stock, so pilots lost not just the stock itself, but the money they'd paid for it, plus what they would have saved in retirement funds during a wild bull market.

One day after a United board meeting, many Chicago-based pilots were standing outside the Chicago headquarters when Glenn Tilton exited. As he passed, the pilots threw their hats on the ground in front him in a gesture of outrage. What I remember most from photos of the event was the look on Tilton's face—pure revulsion. Since that day, the vast majority of United Airlines pilots have never put their hats on again. It was and is the only way we had to make a statement of our solidarity against inhumane management and all cases of corporate callousness and self-interest. You can't fight and win against the executives in large corporations in the United States today. But you can stand up for your principles, even if you can only do it with a hat.

Most of the pilots were in agreement with the hat gesture, but in all such cases, there's at least one person who feels compelled to object. Enter Captain "Hat Nazi."

The official dress code at United required that pilots wear a hat and tie with their uniforms. This does not affect most pilots, who remain hatless in defiant disapproval of the way employees were treated and all they lost. Most wear the tie, but to this day few wear the hat. The "Hat Nazi" is one of those few. So incensed was he by this sign of retaliation on the part of his fellow pilots that he developed a fanatical obsession with hat and tie issues, an obsession he projects on everyone under his command.

I've never met the Hat Nazi, but I've heard countless stories about him, mostly from first officers. I've heard that whenever his first officer isn't wearing a hat, that poor copilot must endure a stern lecture, at the minimum. Once, when a first officer wasn't wearing a tie, the captain left the airplane, walked across the terminal to our flight planning center, purchased a tie, the price of which he deducted from the first officer's pay, and returned to the cockpit insisting the first officer wear it.

The first officer was so angry that the captain had unilaterally decided to debit his account that he refused to fly with him ever again. The tie fracas couldn't have been more pointless—we took our ties off once we were in the cockpit anyway because no one was going to see us for at least twelve hours.

At the time the tie incident was unfolding, the plane reportedly was due to push back from the gate, and a Lufthansa plane was sitting on the ramp with all four engines running, waiting for the same gate. The United airplane pushed back from the gate forty minutes late, thus incurring a $40,000 fine for United. After they completed their trip, the Hat Nazi and the first officer were summoned for an evaluation, and in the end, it was decided that the captain acted in accordance with United's uniform policy. As for his questionable style of conflict resolution, he was told to rein it in a little bit. The first officer, meanwhile, was assigned additional training in our CRM (command leadership, and resource management) program.

It was never in question as to whether the captain had company policy on his side, but that was not the issue to his fellow pilots. It was his belligerence, extremism, and lack of alignment with the principles that affected everyone in the group. To me, it's curious how some people can be so out of sync with a majority, all with common interests, and how unaware or indifferent they can be to their lack of kinship. I also find it mysterious how people can develop certain psychological obsessions, some of them petty. I do know, however, that it's not worth wasting energy trying to figure it out unless one is a psychologist. For the rest of us, the best policy seems to be to accept that we can do nothing about it, try as much as possible to detach ourselves from their behaviors, and be grateful that the only Nazis we're dealing with are hat Nazis.

The Hat Nazi is on the extreme end of the spectrum when it comes to the differences in personalities among pilots. Most differences are within the "normal" range, and although they make for interesting moments in the cockpit and on layovers, they seldom create real problems. When it comes to layovers, two basic personality types emerge—the introvert and the extrovert.

After crews have checked into a hotel, some pilots will go to their room, never to be seen again until pickup the next day. We called those pilots "slam-clickers" because all you hear is the slam of their door and the click of their lock. This can make for a boring layover if you like doing things with other people, although I do understand that some pilots have stressful lives at home, and a layover is an opportunity to be alone and "decompress." I have sometimes used layovers for solitude. Over the years I've utilized that time to acquire both a stockbroker's license and a certified financial planner's license, each of which took me two years. When my wife and I started a furniture business, I spent three months on layovers populating my accounting software with the entire inventory with which we'd started the business. During those phases, I put practical goals ahead of camaraderie while on layovers. But when other goals didn't demand my time, I enjoyed the opportunity to spend time with my fellow pilots, and to explore and appreciate our differences. I've had discussions with pilots of every kind of political view and every philosophical perspective. I've been engaged in religious conversations with pilots who were born-again Christians, Jehovah's Witnesses, and Buddhists. These days I try to avoid such topics because they're so often inflammatory, but in many cases, they led instead to deeper understanding and connection.

It's perhaps more important for pilots to develop this camaraderie than other professionals, because we're captive audiences for each other for many hours at a time, crammed close together in what we call "the aluminum tube." To maintain a sense of harmony and unity, it benefits us to overcome our naturally stoic natures, and also to be tolerant of our differences. After all, in the final analysis, and from a universal perspective, we're really all just as connected as a wing is connected to a fuselage. It may only be connected by three nuts and bolts, but they're specialized, supersized nuts and bolts. It's in our best interest not to do a one-eighty and deviate back to our different backgrounds and upbringings, which breeds judgment or lack of patience with others. This is true not just for pilots, but for flight attendants and the passengers packed into three closely spaced, no leg-room seats, whether in a narrow-body or wide-body plane.

It takes twenty-one days to change a habit, some experts say, including the habit of being judgmental or creating hurtful nicknames. I think of it as three weeks of training, which is only half as long as a full six-week transition course when re-training on a new airplane. Not so bad.

But I'm still working on the Hat Nazi.

CHAPTER TWENTY-SIX
THE LOT OF THE HOMELESS PILOT

Long-distance commutes are a way of life for an airline pilot, so we tend to have a wide variety of living arrangements. Some own condos in the city in which they're based, while others rent apartments or rooms in other people's homes, or in investment homes owned by other crewmembers.

When I was based at LAX (Los Angeles International Airport), I came in for a landing once and noticed a massive employee parking lot with an unusually high number of RVs just short of the approach end of the runway. When I asked a local to explain this to me, I was told that a lot of pilots lived in those RVs. I couldn't help but think of trolls living under bridges, and I found myself wondering: What could have happened in a pilot's life to land him in an RV in the employee parking lot at an international airport?

The answer, I realized, depends on the pilot. In some cases, the pilot is a family man who already owns an RV for vacation purposes and saves on commuting expenses by parking it at the airport where it can double as his home away from home. Another pilot, who may be divorced, might live in an RV out of economic necessity. Sadly, I've heard that there are more of the latter than the former. Then there are just the curveballs of life, the series of events beyond our control where we suddenly find ourselves in a position we could never have imagined. If there was ever a time like that in this century, it was surely 9/11, and then again seven years later with the economic crash of 2008. Not many people saw either of those coming.

In conversations I've had with first officers, I've learned of another denizen of the RV parking lot—the captain who lived beyond his means, which seems to be a sizeable group in the airline industry. I would have thought it more likely for lower-paid first officers to be in that position, but perhaps a captain who makes more also spends more. A life of spending, an expensive divorce, and there they are in a motorhome with a view of incoming 747s. I find it almost tragic that a pilot could end up in an RV in an LAX parking lot, but many do.

The pension and pay cuts at United didn't help; many pilots lived in that lot out of necessity and through no fault of their own. Is there even such a thing as no fault, and do we always get exactly what we've earned? It makes me ponder the law of unintended consequences, which is the principle that nearly everything we do has a consequence attached, whether we're aware of the connection or not. For example, the divorced pilot who finds himself in the parking lot could be facing the consequence of an unwise choice in a marriage partner, even if that decision was made twenty years earlier. All I know is that regardless of what we do, somewhere along the line the law of unintended consequences seems to catch up with us.

Shortly after I discovered the RV lot, I noticed during a landing that most of the RVs were suddenly gone. My first officer told me that the Port Authority of Los Angeles had kicked the RVs out, rather like the police occasionally do a sweep of the homeless in a downtown area. I never found out where the winds of war had scattered these pilots, but I would guess to the closest RV park or camping ground. Wherever they went, they soon returned. Over time, I noticed the RVs popping up again until the lot was eventually as full as it had been.

Although most pilots don't end up in parking lots, all of us have vagabond phases. It's part of paying the dues. When I was in my thirties, I shared crash pads with other pilots, which was something like college dorm living, except I had my own room in a three- or four-bedroom house. Pilots were constantly rotating in and out of these pads at different hours, which worked fine until I hit my forties and needed something more stable. Even today, this isn't an uncommon lifestyle for a pilot who commutes to work. For this and many other reasons, I felt only compassion for the RV pilots. I was advised once to never make fun of anybody in a less fortunate position because you can easily find yourself spiraling down and passing him on his way back up.

I have special sympathy for some other pilots. Often, it's an older first officer who's divorced and lonely, sometimes the result of having been completely wrapped up in his work. As in many professions, some pilots see their work as their sole identity and not simply a way to earn a living. These tend to be the same types who take retirement very hard and have trouble figuring out how to stay productive once the job is gone. Retirement after a lifetime in the workforce can be traumatic, according to some studies. A shocking number of people die within three years of retirement, and idleness and loss of purpose often play a role. Statistics like these keep me motivated to stay involved in extracurricular pursuits. I believe human beings are psychologically designed to have a goal to strive for, and that they live longer when engaged in something meaningful and productive. Maybe that's why most of our Founding Fathers lived beyond the average lifespan of their times, including Benjamin Franklin who reached the then extraordinary age of 84 and signed the U.S. Constitution when he was 81.

This awareness of the importance of purpose helped me prepare for the eventuality of retirement. Among other things, I've developed a passion for music, specifically the acoustic guitar. I started studying music theory so I could understand beautiful and complex compositions, I believe there's magic in being passionate about a cause or interest.

Sitting in a 747 cockpit with my first officer

Acknowledgments

I would like to gratefully acknowledge and thank several people who helped make this book possible.

First my sister Karen Kaye, who offered advice, encouragement, and support during the many years it took me to complete the book. Your patience is amazing.

And Nancy Barton, who guided me in the early development of the book.

And Judith Nielsen, who helped shape and rearrange my original manuscript into a real book.

And John Cannon, whose professionalism, literary expertise and attention to detail were invaluable in preparing the final draft of the manuscript.

And Karen Zatt, my significant other, who helped me get over the finish line.

Photography Credits

Sources for the photographs in this book, listed in order of appearance:

Book cover photo. Photo courtesy of Kenneth Hoke

Standing inside a 747 engine. Photo provided by Scott Kaye

Runway 28R San Francisco International Airport. Gokhan KIRCA/ Shutterstock.com

United 747 taxiing. Stonemeadow Photography/ Alamy stock photo

747 thrust levers. iStock.com/aroundtheworld.photography

747 lifting off Runway 28R. Plane Photography/Shutterstock.com

United 747 climbing after takeoff. Vytautas Kielaitis/Shutterstock.com

The green flash. iStock.com/Paul Wilson

Learjet climbing. Fasttailwind/Shutterstock.com

Cort Aviation promotional poster. Photo by Scott Kaye

757—sleek and sexy. A Periam Photography/Shutterstock.com

Vile Vortice whirlpool. Photo Junction/Shutterstock.com

Cessna 310. Aviation Images/ Alamy stock photo

Baby chicks in a crate. iStock.com/Ryan JLane

Denver Rocky Mountain front range. John De Bond/Shutterstock.com

Rocky Mountain overflight. iStock.com/Rallek

Lenticular cloud. iStock.com/chuvipro

Contrails. Egmont Elsner/Shutterstock.com

Contrail patterns. iStock.com/santosha

Routing of AirAsia 8501. Xinhua/ Alamy stock photo

Recovered wreckage of AirAsia 8501. US Navy Photo/ Alamy stock photo

Jackson Hole, Wyoming, precarious takeoff. Ken Schulze/Shutterstock.com

Sitting in a 747 cockpit with my first officer. Photo provided by Scott Kaye

CPSIA information can be obtained
at www.ICGtesting.com
Printed in the USA
BVHW060508250919

559309BV00003B/7/P